HOMESCHOOLING
THE CHILD WITH *ADD*
(OR OTHER
SPECIAL *NEEDS*)

LENORE COLACION HAYES

Linda Dobson, Series Editor

HOMESCHOOLING THE CHILD WITH *ADD* (OR OTHER SPECIAL *N*EEDS)

YOUR COMPLETE GUIDE TO SUCCESSFULLY HOMESCHOOLING THE CHILD WITH LEARNING DIFFERENCES

PRIMA PUBLISHING

Published by Prima Publishing, Roseville, California. Member of the Crown Publishing Group, a division of Random House, Inc.

PRIMA PUBLISHING and colophon are trademarks of Random House, Inc., registered with the United States Patent and Trademark Office.

Library of Congress Cataloging-in-Publication Data on File
  ISBN 0-7615-3569-1

02 03 04 05 DD 10 9 8 7 6 5 4 3 2 1
Printed in the United States of America

First Edition

Visit us online at www.primapublishing.com

Get more out of your GMAT® Official Guides!

ONLINE

**Visit gmat.wiley.com to get free online access
to the same questions in this guide**

- Build your own practice sets based on difficulty and question type
- View performance metrics to help you focus your study
- Practice pacing and time management in exam mode

Go to gmat.wiley.com

Create an account and enter the access code on the
inside front cover of this book

For customer support, please visit http://wileyactual.com/gmat/help

To my son, Nigel "Poncho" Ott,
whose empathic intuitiveness and wicked sense
of humor keep life balanced for me

CONTENTS

ACKNOWLEDGMENTS

I WISH TO extend my heartfelt appreciation to the many families who opened their lives to me during the writing of this book. They freely discussed their joys and challenges, so that newcomers to homeschooling could share in the benefit of hindsight. I'm glad that I've gotten to know so many of you—you've all truly touched my life.

Loving indebtedness goes to Bob, my life partner and best friend, for his unwavering support and love. I'm blessed with a husband who is an excellent cook, so we didn't have to resort to take-out food while I worked on this book. My son deserves kudos for his loving patience.

Enormous gratitude goes to my son's medical and mental health professionals. These dedicated individuals treated him with respect and understanding, while providing his worried parents with guidance and assurance. I don't know how we would have "survived" the early years without Nord Nation, M.D., Ann Nation, R.N., and Charles G. O'Malley, Ph.D. An extra special hug also goes to Vi Olguin for her early support and friendship. Our current "team" of Deborah Pauer, M.D., Ray Brady, D.D.S., and Matthew Cramer, D.C., has helped to guide Nigel through adolescence and into adulthood.

My number one nurturing award goes to Dr. Betty Cuichta for keeping my body, soul, and mind calmed and focused through the years, especially while I worked on this project.

Sincere appreciation goes to my two cats, Figgie Rose and Max, for the long hours they kept me company at the computer.

Thank you to Linda Dobson and Jamie Miller for providing me with the opportunity to write this book, and to Tara Mead for her editing expertise and unflappable patience.

Finally, my deepest gratitude and love go to the late Janie Levine Hellyer, who was the one to first illustrate to me that square-peg-in-round-hole children learn best at home.

INTRODUCTION

*T*HE U.S. DEPARTMENT of Education estimates that nearly forty-seven million students are currently enrolled in public schools. Approximately six million of these children are receiving special education services. Countless others are struggling in classrooms without assistance, either because their needs have not yet been identified or because their learning difficulties do not meet the qualifying guidelines for special education. Unfortunately, qualifying for public school services does not guarantee a quality or even mediocre education. The federal government mandates a free and appropriate public education for all children. Yet when federal funding pays a paltry 15 percent toward state special education programs, it's no wonder that so many children are left behind.

It is a daily struggle for the average child to get an education when classrooms are overcrowded, learning materials are outdated, and overworked teachers have been reduced to college-educated child care providers. For those children who are in any way different from the norm, it is virtually impossible to learn in such a chaotic and unforgiving environment.

By the fact that this book is in your hands, you must agree, at least in part, that traditional schooling is not meeting the needs of children—*your children*. Perhaps you are a parent whose child has been diagnosed with an emotional or learning disorder. Or possibly a diagnosis for your child has not been reached, but you have suspicions that all is not "right" with your child. Or maybe your child has a physical difference or health condition that has been diagnosed but that requires some type of special school accommodations. Or it could be that your child is not yet of school age, but you are wondering how his spirited nature will fare in a classroom setting. Whatever your situation, you are most likely reaching the end of your rope in terms of your child's school situation.

If you are reading this book, then you are probably contemplating homeschooling your child. Regardless of which path brought you to homeschooling, you are not alone. A 1999 study conducted by the U.S. Department of Education estimated that nearly a million children, approximately 2 percent of K–12 students, are being educated at home. Although these figures might not seem overwhelmingly in favor of homeschooling, it is notable that the ranks are swelling at an annual rate of 11 percent. According to the study, parents reported numerous reasons for opting out of institutionalized education—poor learning environment, safety concerns, school behavior problems, and inability to address child's special needs, to name only a few. Overall, the majority of parents simply felt they could provide a better education at home.

Thirteen years ago, my family joined the small but growing population of homeschoolers. I wish I could say that we chose to participate in the home education movement based on a philosophical notion to reform the educational system. But that wasn't our original intent. We came to homeschooling by default. Our son had the dubious honor of having been asked to leave three part-time preschool settings by his fourth birthday. His crime? Nonconformity. The standard preschool environment calls for children to change activities approximately every fifteen minutes, which is the average attention span of children aged two through five. My son would just be warming up to a new activity when he would be pulled away for an entirely new experience. When he was unable to convey his frustration to his teachers, he would resort to screaming meltdowns. The early childhood specialists who staffed these programs warned us that our son most likely had Attention Deficit Disorder (ADD) or autism and advised that we rush him into treatment to prepare him for the school environment he'd be facing in one short year.

We took these concerns to our son's pediatrician, who indicated that he saw our son as a bright, happy, and spirited child, but possibly a late-bloomer in some academic areas. The doctor encouraged us to continue whatever it was we were doing to nurture our son's growth. While we were relieved to receive this news, we continued to struggle with "Are we doing the right thing for our son?" The pediatrician referred us for a second opinion to a psychologist who specialized in behavior problems in boys. After a few months of weekly sessions, the psychologist proclaimed our son intelligent, content, and difficult in temperament. He felt that our son could be "at risk" for ADD due to a family history, but he was reluctant to issue a formal diagnosis for such a young child. He cautioned us that placing our son in a traditional school would be like forcing a square peg into a round hole. The psychologist offered to work as a partner with our family and our son's future school settings to help ease his passage into the classroom.

We felt that private schools would be our best option given that most claimed to have low student-teacher ratios and a policy of embracing individuals. After visiting countless private schools within a two-hour driving radius of our home, however, I didn't see much difference from public schools, except that the private ones came with a hefty price tag. All of the private schools were unwilling to take a hands-on approach with a spirited and socially immature child, even with the offer of assistance from his psychologist.

Public school was definitely not an option for our son. At the time he was to start kindergarten, I was in graduate school pursuing studies in psychology and education, while also training to be an elementary school counselor at the public school. My experiences in that school opened my eyes to what my son would have to endure. Children who were timid or different in any manner were subjected to taunting by their peers and, in many cases, poor treatment by their teachers. I watched as numerous children made their afternoon trek to the nurse's office for a dose of psychostimulant medication, which was generally administered by a school secretary because there wasn't funding for a full-time nurse. I was appalled that young children of color were automatically assumed to be lacking in intelligence and character. Once many of my colleagues realized that I was biracial, the overt racism stopped; but I knew it had only gone underground in my presence.

My husband and I felt stuck, without options for our son's educational future. We announced to anyone who asked that we were going to delay kindergarten. We realized a year was not going to magically make a difference in our son's school readiness, but at least it would buy us additional time to look for private schools. I was certain that there had to be a program somewhere that would meet my son's needs. We finally found it—at home!

Despite our initial status as "default" homeschoolers, we have, through the years, wholeheartedly embraced it as a viable educational alternative. That once elusive diagnosis for our son no longer mattered because we had the freedom to work with his differences and make adjustments as needed. There was no need to publicly place his weaknesses under the microscope of school administrators. We never had to jump through bureaucratic hoops to obtain what we needed for our son's education. As a one-income family, we were able to create a vibrant learning environment using library books, art supplies, field trips, and other low-cost resources.

Homeschooling has been very beneficial for my square-peg-in-round-hole son. But the dedicated parent advocate doesn't make a life-altering decision based solely on one opinion, so in this book I've brought together approximately forty other special needs homeschoolers to share their experiences. In early 2001, I posted queries to numerous e-mail lists, searching for those who homeschool learning disabled or other special needs children. More than sixty families responded and completed an online questionnaire. In some cases, I was able to glean enough information from individual questionnaires; in other cases, I communicated further with the families about their homeschooling lives. The families who participated in this project spanned the homeschooling continuum:

- ✦ Veteran homeschoolers (two or more years) outnumbered the newcomers (one year or less) by two to one.

- ✦ Families hailed from twenty different states, with one respondent from outside of the United States.

- ✦ Children ranged in age from preschoolers (some who had been enrolled in early intervention public school programs) to young adults (who had been homeschooled and are now finished).

- ✦ The majority of these children had attended traditional school (either public or private) and came to homeschooling when their educational/emotional needs were not being met.

- ✦ Approximately one-third of the children had always been homeschooled.

- ✦ Some parents had already been homeschooling neurotypical (NT) or "normal" children, but felt unable to meet the needs of their special children.

- ✦ Other families, after seeing the successes of homeschooling their differently abled children, have removed their NT children from school to homeschool.

- ✦ Nearly all of the children have received a formal diagnosis of a learning, psychological, or physical disorder. The remaining children are suspected of possessing some "difference," but have not been diagnosed by a licensed professional.

- ✦ The most common diagnoses included ADD/ADHD, disorders on the autism spectrum (including Asperger's Syndrome and pervasive developmental disorders), and learning or communicative disorders. Many of the children have multiple diagnoses, including giftedness.

Do these descriptors sound similar to your own family? Do you want to provide your children with a loving, personally tailored environment in which they can learn? If so, then this book will help pave your path as you enter into educating your own children.

Part one of this book examines how more and more children are being diagnosed with a variety of disorders that seem to be preventing learning. The prevailing thought is that biochemical and genetic disorders interfere with the cognitive and emotional development in these children, thus hindering their ability to function within a classroom with same-age peers. Many medical and mental health professionals, however, are looking to another component responsible for a child's inability to learn—traditional schooling with its standardized curriculum and other practices that do not encourage individual strengths.

The first part also discusses the various childhood disorders that are commonly diagnosed. Although many individuals (children and adults) do possess learning, physical, and emotional difficulties, there are just as many children who are needlessly diagnosed with serious psychopathology simply because they're late-bloomers or possess some other type of unique difference. Adults appear to expect more of children at earlier ages, both academically and emotionally. These assumptions contribute to the high incidence of troubled children and school failures.

Part two addresses the issues that define quality teachers and whether noncertified parents are qualified to educate their special needs children. Homeschoolers discuss how they approached these concerns and how they continue to build confidence. (The names of many of the subjects quoted in this book have been changed to protect their identity.)

Part two also examines the reasons that parents chose homeschooling over traditional schooling. Most parents simply grew tired of fighting with school officials for desperately needed services to help their children succeed academically. Many parents found their children developing stress-related depression and anxieties because of the ongoing struggles to keep up with their classmates. Overall, families feel that their children have been abandoned by traditional education.

Many homeschoolers have found success by working toward their children's strengths rather than the common practice of overfocusing on weaknesses. One chapter in part two looks at Harvard psychologist Howard Gardner's theory of multiple intelligences and how homeschoolers have found it useful in working with their differently abled children. This, along with the myriad homeschooling styles, has afforded many families with the knowledge and ability to teach their own.

Part two also contains suggestions for dealing with family and friends who have not wholeheartedly embraced your homeschooling, as well as a section on meeting the needs of your other children, your spouse, and yourself.

The nuts and bolts of homeschooling your differently abled child is the focus of part three. Starting with an examination of what homeschoolers refer to as the dreaded "S" question: "What about socialization?" Included are tips on what to look for in homeschooling support systems for yourself and your children and steps to take if you're starting your own group.

A chapter on choosing learning materials for your homeschool includes an exhaustive list of homeschooling veterans' favorite picks of curricula, books, Web sites, and other helpful resources.

The pros and cons of using limited public school services as a homeschooler is also explored in part three. In addition, ideas for other treatment options, including suggestions for locating homeschool-friendly service providers, are discussed. The book concludes with final encouragements from respondent families.

What is contained in this book is only a sampling of experiences and ideas. I am always searching for helpful resources and update my homeschooling special needs Web site (www.bayshoreeducational.com/special.html) regularly with new information and insights.

Homeschooling isn't a panacea to cure all ills, but it is a viable option that provides an enormous amount of flexibility to educate your children. It is possible for the disabled, disordered, or just plain different child to learn and thrive in an environment that isn't restricted to "dumbed-down" content or that requires parental adeptness in bureaucratic hoop-jumping. Take one step at a time. Using this book as a guide, you'll have the wisdom of many homeschooling mothers, and a few fathers, illuminating your path.

Homeschooling the Child with ADD (or Other Special Needs)

1

WHAT'S WRONG
WITH MY CHILD?

In This Chapter

✦ The school experience for differently abled children

✦ Why is my child not learning in school?

✦ Homeschooling as a viable alternative

✦ Home from school

✦ Never crossed the threshold of a classroom

*T*HERE'S SOMETHING WRONG with your child.

These dreaded words strike anguish in countless parents. For many families, the knowledge that something is not "normal" about their child comes shortly after birth when doctors detect some type of abnormality. Other families will assume normal development until the child enters school and experiences difficulties learning within a classroom setting. Still other families realize their child is somehow "different," yet a concrete diagnosis eludes them. All share a common bond: Once a medical, mental health, or educational professional utters those words, life as the family once knew it will never be the same.

At this point, the family of the "different" child will begin a fact-finding odyssey. What exactly is wrong with my child? What caused this condition? Was this brought on by something we did or did not do as parents? Is there a cure? How will our child learn in school? Parents will pose these questions (and many, many others) to their children's teachers and pediatricians, who in turn, will provide referrals to more specialized practitioners, such as psychologists, family therapists, and speech and occupational therapists.

From that point on, the families have entered the world of what can be referred to as the "differently abled." This term is one intended to counter the negative connotations of "disabled," which implies that because a person is different, he or she is inferior. The use of the term "differently abled" represents a plea to society to discard longstanding negative notions regarding individual abilities.

THE SCHOOL EXPERIENCE FOR DIFFERENTLY ABLED CHILDREN

LEARNING DISABLED AND special needs children are generally educated in public schools or federally funded programs that provide remediation and speech, occupational, or other therapies. In 1975, the U.S. government passed the first public law mandating that all identified children will be provided with a free appropriate public education (FAPE). This is now known as the Individuals with Disabilities Education Act (IDEA). Unfortunately, most schools do not receive full government funding for their special education or resource programs. Families with more discretionary income can bypass or augment the public services and turn to private professionals. But many simply do not have this choice. As a result, many children do not receive the assistance needed to facilitate learning. Many families pursue legal action to force school districts to provide all mandated services. Judges do order schools to make such services available, even if it means local districts must foot the bill for private therapists or tutors. But lawsuits are costly and time-consuming efforts that offer no guarantees and that often take an emotional toll on already stressed families trying to cope with children in need.

WHY IS MY CHILD NOT LEARNING IN SCHOOL?

A PREVALENT THOUGHT as to why children experience learning difficulties is that they have some type of biochemical or genetic disorder that prevents normal cognitive, physical, and emotional development. Recently, however, a strong belief has emerged among a growing minority of medical and mental health professionals that an entirely different reason explains why there is a growing number of children with learning difficulties. It isn't that children are unable to learn but that many are unnecessarily labeled with learning disorders simply because they don't perform academically at or above levels similar to peers of the same age.

In previous generations, parents, teachers, and doctors generally looked to child development guidelines as templates for gauging a child's progress along a continuum of growth. If a child's ability to read were a bit delayed, the adults in her life would take a wait-and-see approach. Educators and parents were willing to offer encouragement and patiently await further maturation. Formal educational or medical intervention only took place after it was clear that "growing out" of the problem wasn't working.

> Many children are unnecessarily labeled with learning disorders simply because they don't perform academically at or above levels similar to peers of the same age.

By current educational standards, however, if a child doesn't read by a prescribed age, he's examined for neurological faults, labeled with a disease, and assigned to a special classroom or service to await his academic doom. It seems that developmental guidelines have been extrapolated to standardize the process of learning.

Development Need Not Be a Deadline

Jean Piaget, the Swiss psychologist, developed what is one of the most noted theories of cognitive development. Basing his conclusions on years of research and observation, Piaget indicated that children are generally able to accomplish certain intellectual tasks at certain ages. Piaget's theories, as well as those developed by other child developmentalists, are based on typical standards for the majority of children studied and are not intended to hold each child accountable for actually being able to read, write, or reason by a predetermined age.

It's obvious that children do not reach the same levels of cognitive, physical, or emotional development at exactly the same age. As parents, from an intellectual perspective, we can comfortably make this statement about children—"Of course! All children develop at different times, and it is completely normal!" But then a well-meaning friend or family member points out that our child isn't reading quite as well as another child of the same age. At that point, our emotions send a jolt to our reasoning, and we end up feeling utterly demoralized about our child and ourselves.

HOMESCHOOLING AS A VIABLE ALTERNATIVE

PARENTS ARE GROWING weary of running around and getting nowhere (much like hamsters on a wheel) searching for the proper diagnosis and treatment, battling with school officials for services to meet the child's needs, while witnessing the life and soul being squeezed out of their once-inquisitive child. Many parents now choose to bypass the public system of services by addressing the needs of their learning disabled and special needs children within the context of the home, family, and community.

These children whose abilities don't mesh with the norm, once miserable within the confines of the classroom, now meet and, in many cases, exceed the academic and emotional expectations of their parents and of professionals.

Cherylynn, a Missouri parent, spent years trying to convince the local school district that the diagnoses given her son when he was a toddler were inaccurate. Because the school provided the referral to a nearby children's hospital, the administrators were unwilling to budge from the mentally retarded diagnosis. Yet Cherylynn knew that her son was bright in spite of his differences. She eventually decided she could no longer allow her son to continue receiving an education she knew to be substandard and withdrew him from school. Cherylynn speaks to the desperation experienced by many families: "We knew nothing about homeschooling when we first pulled our son out of school. We only knew he was in a very harmful situation, and we had to get him out." Years passed, and Cherylynn's son thrived as he learned outside of a classroom, as have her four younger always-homeschooled children, two of which also have learning differences.

As her son readied himself for college, Cherylynn took him to a large university medical center, where he received a more realistic diagnosis of Asperger's Syndrome, a form of autism. This diagnosis verified Cherylynn's convictions that her son possessed the ability to lead a life in which he functioned at a relatively high level—a conviction further proven by his current university studies.

Meeting Individual Needs

Homeschooling has many advantages in general, but it is especially valuable for a child who is not a good "fit" with school. Parents can tailor learning experiences to address the needs of a child who reads at an eighth grade level, does math at a fourth grade level, and writes at a sixth grade level. Homeschoolers are not confined to grade levels because children freely learn at their own pace.

One-to-One Learning

One aspect of special education that professionals and parents agree on is that children experience more learning successes when interacting with teachers one-to-one (or close to it). Schools simply cannot accommodate such a low adult-to-child ratio, but parents can when they educate their own children.

> Schools simply cannot accommodate a one-to-one adult-to-child ratio, but parents can when they educate their own children.

Flexible Pace

Parenting a child with different abilities is almost always a difficult task in and of itself. Family life is strained further when daily homework assignments enter the mix. Many parents report that volatile outbursts, once common in their households, greatly diminish when the family and child take control of their studies. Homeschooling allows children the freedom to work at an individual pace and, in many cases, to provide input as to what they wish to learn and how they will approach the material. Tamara, a parent in California, experienced this with her always-homeschooled ten-year-old son: "My son can't do long seatwork and needs frequent breaks. Because of oppositional defiant disorder (ODD), there's a need for a lot of compromise. He needs to feel a sense of victory over choosing what to read or what subject to do before another. Homeschooling provides that flexibility."

Different Styles, Intelligences, and Strengths

Harvard psychologist Howard Gardner theorized that schools traditionally teach to those children who have strong verbal and math skills. This neglects those children who draw on other abilities to learn. In his book, *Frames of Mind,* Gardner outlined his theory of seven intelligences (a few years later, he added an eighth intelligence) by which individuals are capable of learning. Chapter 5 examines the theory of multiple intelligences and how it pertains to home educators. It is a theory that many homeschoolers find useful in understanding and working with their children.

"Since I understand her learning style and strengths, we have created a program that focuses on what she *can do*, instead of obsessing over her weaknesses," says Alaskan homeschooling parent, Tammy, about her eleven-year-old autistic daughter. "The more we inspire her to succeed through her strengths, the better she does in her weak areas. If a program is not working, we can tweak it or find something better. I have the time to develop a curriculum to fit her, not force her into a program that doesn't fit."

Social and Behavioral Benefits

Another advantage of homeschooling is that homeschooled children with slight to moderate learning differences are not subject to placement in special education classes where they frequently adopt the behaviors of students with more serious disorders. The homeschooled child can learn appropriate life skills from those with a vested interest in seeing him succeed—the family and the community at large.

The inability to develop proper social skills is an area of concern for parents and differently abled children, especially those with developmental disorders. These children frequently appear shy or immature because they lack the ability to pick up social cues and tend to be overwhelmed by large groups of people. These abilities are integral to life in the classroom or on the playground. Teachers and school counselors simply do not have enough time to help these children become socially adept. But homeschooling parents can work with their children, assisting them in identifying proper social cues and standards within smaller groups, such as the family, the child's neighborhood

HOW WE DID IT

I've been homeschooling my son Nick for most of his thirteen years, initially because he was too medically fragile to go to school. I spent most of my time learning about Nick's medical needs and not a lot of time toward real teaching because I felt I lacked the preparation and skills. I looked forward to when he would be able to attend school outside our home so he could receive the help of the professional school staff.

Yet when Nick finally entered school, I learned the limits of the system and how unthrilled they were with my child. I was devastated. I fought to get what Nick needed, meeting brick walls at every turn. Nick is deaf, has facial anomalies, a seizure disorder, and a tracheotomy tube. The school placed him in a physically or otherwise health-impaired program (POHI). Yet he wasn't even offered speech therapy.

In 1999, a truck hit Nick. It was the worst and best day of his life to date. Nick suffered head trauma, the near loss of one leg, and loss of his permanent teeth.

buddies, and homeschooling support groups. As Tammy states, "Socialization in schools for autistic children is like drinking water with a fire hose. The kids feel so bombarded; they either shut down mentally or lash out with poor behaviors. Homeschooling allows our daughter to enjoy people who are a variety of ages, not just her peers, which is a very narrow sliver of humanity."

HOME FROM SCHOOL

HOMESCHOOLING VETERANS GENERALLY advise those who are moving from traditional schooling to homeschooling to allow at

During his recovery, I was faced with the dilemma—give him psychotropic drugs so he could cope within the school setting or teach him myself.

I wasn't encouraged with our homeschooling at first, but the benefits are now apparent. Nick is medication-free and making excellent academic progress. I also taught him to eat (orally) when no one thought he could.

Every Sunday, I read the local paper and map out the events we can participate in during the coming week. When Nick was in formal school, he wasn't allowed to participate in field trips. Now he goes all over—to the zoo, art museums, and the science center.

I use the Internet, as well as the ideas of many doctors, therapists, and friends, to find learning activities. I tend to take whatever interest Nick has in the world around him and run with it. We do science experiments and lots of hands-on learning.

This kind of schooling takes a huge commitment, but it's worth it. At home, Nick is much healthier and happier, and he learns better in an environment free from the classroom stimuli. Homeschooling works for us!

—MARY, HOMESCHOOLING PARENT IN MICHIGAN

least one month to "detox" or de-school for each year enrolled in traditional school. This means letting go of schoolish notions and getting on with the business of life and learning at one's own pace.

Time for Healing and Growth

The child who has learning differences, however, may need additional time to heal from his school experiences. It is difficult enough for a child to have accomplished little to no academic success, but to also endure tortuous teasing from classmates can leave a child's sense of self-worth fractured. Although they view academics as important, many homeschooling families prefer to focus initially on restoring physical and emotional well-being to their children, and they often report reaping the benefits rather quickly.

"She is calmer, healthier," says Lisa, a Michigan parent, of her fifteen-year-old daughter, who has autism and epilepsy and has been homeschooled for six years. "She exceeded the school's lifetime expectations within six months, and our whole family is happier. I no longer have to fight for what she needs, we just work on it."

> "Socialization in schools for autistic children is like drinking water with a fire hose."

Beryl, a Michigan parent, has an autistic daughter who was experiencing language delays. The family had initially placed the daughter in an early intervention public school program. They then decided to delay enrollment in kindergarten because they were moving out of the area. Beryl reminisces about those days four years ago: "I figured, why not try homeschooling for the next few months before she enrolled in kindergarten. Within six weeks, she began accomplishing goals that she never came close to reaching in the 'early intervention' preschool. That was all it took to convince me that this was the way to go."

NEVER CROSSED THE THRESHOLD OF A CLASSROOM

SOME PARENTS REALIZE very early in their children's lives that school is not in the future. "My fifteen-year-old son has never been to school. Sitting still that long would kill him," states LJ of Oregon. "He learned to read around age eleven or twelve and never felt any 'difference.' He is a favorite among all the adults he meets, and he gets along well with other kids. My son has never been diagnosed," she admits, "but our doctor will do so, if and when a diagnosis is ever necessary. I feel that adults have the power, and therefore the responsibility, to meet the needs of the child—with or without a label."

My now eighteen-year-old son also never attended school. After the psychologist told us that placing Nigel in school would be like trying to force a square peg into a round hole, we didn't even consider it an option. Given his difficult temperament, we knew school attendance would only create further problems in an already chaotic life with a difficult child.

At this point, you may be wondering, "Can I actually educate my own differently abled child?" Most certainly! To date, no formal studies have been done to substantiate the position that homeschooling is beneficial for children with learning disorders or other special needs. However, innumerable personal accounts from homeschooling families point toward success. After all, special education laws dictate that a child with special needs be placed in the least restrictive environment. What could be less restrictive than homeschooling?

SIMPLE STARTING POINTS

✦ *Read homeschooling books and publications.* Many public libraries have homeschool resource manuals available in the reference section (often thanks to the efforts of local support groups). Also, retail bookstores now stock many homeschooling titles and periodicals.

✦ *Search Internet resources.* Enter "homeschooling" and your state of residence as search terms into a favorite search engine to locate general and local information. Most state homeschooling organizations are treasure troves packed with legal requirements, e-mail lists (join and ask lots of questions), and links to other helpful resources.

✦ *Daydream.* About your family's future! Think back to the lazy days of school vacations when you weren't prodding your child to get out of bed on time or complete his homework. Remember how those days were less hectic and how you and your child had more time to delve into interesting activities. Think about how your family will pursue passions as you become involved in your new learning environment. Homeschooling won't magically make your troubles disappear, but it will make life more manageable.

✦ *Maintain restraint.* Homeschooling sounds exactly like what your child needs. You're excited at the prospect of reclaiming your family, and you want to share your news! Tread this path cautiously. Well-meaning family and friends, unfamiliar with homeschooling, may try to dissuade you. Take time to learn everything you can about homeschooling and join e-mail lists to develop a support network. It will be easier to deflect objections when you're well prepared to respond with knowledge and confidence.

RESOURCES

Books

Briggs, Dorothy Corkille. *Your Child's Self-Esteem: Step-by-Step Guidelines for Raising Responsible, Productive, Happy Children.* Doubleday, 1975.

Dobson, Linda (ed.). *The Homeschooling Book of Answers: The 88 Most Important Questions Answered by Homeschooling's Most Respected Voices.* Prima Publishing, 1998.

Elkind, David. *The Hurried Child: Growing Up Too Fast Too Soon.* Perseus Press, 1989.

Elkind, David. *Miseducation: Preschoolers at Risk.* Knopf, 1988.

Elkind, David. *Sympathetic Understanding of the Child: Birth to Sixteen.* 3d ed. Allyn & Bacon, 1994.

Gardner, Howard. *Frames of Mind: The Theory of Multiple Intelligences.* Basic Books, 1993.

Gatto, John Taylor. *Dumbing Us Down: The Hidden Curriculum of Compulsory Schooling.* New Society Publishers, 1991.

Gatto, John Taylor. *The Underground History of American Education: A Schoolteacher's Intimate Investigation into the Problem of Modern Schooling.* The Oxford Village Press, 2000.

Griffith, Mary. *The Homeschooling Handbook.* 2d ed. Prima Publishing, 1999.

Hensley, Sharon. *Homeschooling Children with Special Needs.* Noble Publishing, 1995.

Holt, John. *Teach Your Own: A Hopeful Path for Education.* Delacourte, 1989. (This book, unfortunately, is out of print but may be available in libraries or used book outlets.)

Kohn, Alfie. *The Schools Our Children Deserve: Moving Beyond Traditional Classrooms and "Tougher Standards."* Mariner Books, 2000.

Markova, Dawna. *No Enemies Within: A Creative Process for Discovering What's Right About What's Wrong.* Conari Press, 1994.

Moore, Raymond S., and Dorothy N. Moore. *Better Late Than Early: A New Approach to Your Child's Education.* Reader's Digest Press, 1982.

Ray, Brian. *Strengths of Their Own: Homeschoolers Across America.* National Home Education Research Institute, 1997.

Rupp, Rebecca. *Getting Started on Home Learning: How and Why to Teach Your Kids at Home.* Three Rivers Press, 1999.

Message Boards

Home Education Magazine: www.home-ed-magazine.com/DSC/discus/index.html

VegSource Discussion Lists: www.vegsource.com/homeschool/

Organizations

Holt Associates, 2380 Massachusetts Avenue, Suite 104, Cambridge, MA 02140, 617-864-3100, www.holtgws.com

NATional cHallenged Homeschoolers Associated Network (NATHHAN), P.O. Box 39, Porthill, ID 83853, 208-267-6246, www.nathhan.com

National Home Education Network (NHEN), P.O. Box 7844, Long Beach, CA 90807, www.nhen.org

National Home Education Research Institute (NHERI), 925 Cottage Street NE, Salem, OR 97309, www.nheri.org

Periodicals

Home Education Magazine (HEM), P.O. Box 1083, Tonasket, WA
98855, 509-486-1351, www.home-ed-magazine.com

Homeschooling Today, P.O. Box 1608, Fort Collins, CO 80522,
904-475-3088, www.homeschooltoday.com

Web Sites

BayShore Homeschoolers' Special Needs Resources: www.bayshore
educational.com/special.html

Homeschooling Kids with Disabilities: members.tripod.com
/~Maaja/index.html

Kaleidoscapes for Kids and Home Education Enthusiasts: www
.kaleidoscapes.com

NHEN Homeschooling Basics: www.nhen.org/nhen/pov/newhser/

Unschooling.com: www.unschooling.com

2

YOUR CHILD'S
DIAGNOSIS

In This Chapter

✦ Disorder du jour

✦ Disorders or normal childhood traits?

✦ Commonly diagnosed childhood learning disorders

✦ Are tests and evaluations really necessary?

✦ Pros and cons of formal diagnosis

OUR SOCIETY HAS a love-hate relationship with the notion of success and failure. On one hand, we advocate that everyone's capable of reaching his or her full potential. On the other hand, we quickly attach labels to those (generally children) who *do* reach for the stars in their own unique style. An adult with boundless energy who's obsessively focused on one area may be viewed as being successful. A child exhibiting similar traits is judged "at-risk" for academic failure.

There are, however, individuals who truly have learning, emotional, and mental problems caused by a variety of origins or circumstances. At one end of the spectrum are mental and physical disabilities related to biochemical or genetic differences or resulting from an accident during birth or later in childhood. Other causes found to impair learning include socioeconomic issues, dietary factors, and environmental allergens. Rounding out the opposite end of the continuum are the learning disorders that seem to have no basis, but the child is still not reaching her full academic potential. This large and growing population of children has been diagnosed with severe psychopathologies simply because they learn or adapt in a manner that differs from the norm.

DISORDER DU JOUR

THERE ARE A number of disorders that are frequently assigned because the diagnostic criteria sort of match a child's behaviors. In many cases, the disorders are already accepted for adult populations but are extrapolated to include children. Popular media educate us about these disorders, while parents and teachers grasp onto them in efforts to make sense of why children struggle in school. The diagnoses of choice include Attention Deficit-Hyperactivity Disorder (ADHD), Oppositional Defiant Disorder (ODD), Asperger's Syndrome, Central Auditional Processing Disorder (CAPD), and Bipolar Disorder, to name only a few.

> These up-and-coming popular diseases seem to serve no purpose other than to create more "alphabet disordered" children.

There is also a burgeoning field of "entrepreneurial disorders" developed and encouraged by both professionals and parent advocates. While many of these labels frequently draw symptoms from actual disorders, other behaviors are added into the mix and new syndromes are born. These up-and-coming popular diseases seem to serve no purpose other than to create more "alphabet disordered" children, while profiting off parents desperate for answers and "cures."

DISORDERS OR NORMAL CHILDHOOD TRAITS?

THERE ARE COMMON traits among many of the more popular childhood disorders—inattentiveness, high activity level, forgetfulness, a tendency to frustrate quickly, and distractibility. These traits are often not due to a brain malfunction, but because many of them are quite normal for children. The real disorders appear to be inappropriate adult expectations and the inability to accept a growing, exploring child's behaviors. Noted psychiatrist Peter R. Breggin, M.D., states in his book *Reclaiming Our Children,* "Children don't have disorders; they live in a disordered world." From a youthful perspective, a chaotic life does certainly seem rational when parents are preoccupied juggling multiple responsibilities, teachers are overwhelmed, and peers think them odd. Who wouldn't act out in such a situation?

Acting out indicates a problem for which the child is usually to blame. As a result, countless scores of active, but otherwise healthy, children are unnecessarily labeled and treated. The preferred treatments for these children include intensive therapies, psychotropic medication, or special classes. Not to discount the untold numbers of individuals who have found these approaches to be life-saving tools, but many of these unjustly labeled children simply need interventions consisting of kindhearted direction, respect, and an abundance of patience from the adults in their lives.

COMMONLY DIAGNOSED CHILDHOOD LEARNING DISORDERS

THE FOLLOWING INFORMATION can help you to examine the most commonly diagnosed childhood disorders. It is not exhaustive nor is it meant to replace a professional assessment. Use this section as a starting point to compare and contrast the various symptoms related to learning difficulties. Keep in mind that individuals possessing any of these behaviors do not necessarily have a learning or emotional disorder.

Mental health difficulties are guided by the Diagnostic and Statistical Manual of Mental Disorders, currently in its fourth edition (DSM-IV). The manual is published and periodically updated by the American Psychiatric Association (APA). The following descriptions are based on APA criteria and professional literature.

Asperger's Syndrome (AS)

The Viennese physician Hans Asperger identified this cluster of symptoms in the 1940s. Since Asperger noted the syndrome, most European countries have accepted it as a pervasive developmental disorder. Not until 1994, however, did the APA officially recognize it. Some refer to it as high-functioning autism, although the two differ in certain ways. Individuals with AS generally possess normal to above-average intelligence and are more capable of developing speech than are people with autism. The principal signs of AS are:

+ Difficulty understanding nonverbal behaviors, such as facial expressions and body language
+ Inability or difficulty developing peer relationships
+ Lack of empathy
+ Repetitive use of language and/or motor movements
+ Preoccupation with specific parts of objects
+ Inflexibility in changing routines

Attention-Deficit/Hyperactivity Disorder (ADHD)

Through the years, ADHD has been referred to by a variety of less-than-flattering terms, including minimal brain dysfunction, hyperkinetic reaction of childhood, and hyperactive child syndrome. The APA officially recognized this pervasive developmental disorder in 1980. The principal signs are:

+ Inability to pay close attention to the task at hand
+ Difficulty organizing tasks
+ Easily distracted
+ Forgetfulness
+ Fidgety or squirmy activity
+ Difficulty playing quietly
+ Difficulty awaiting turn
+ Tendency to interrupt others
+ Excessive talking
+ Appearance of being "motor driven"

According to the DSM-IV, a child receiving the diagnosis of ADHD must be overly active and have a short attention span.

The child with only an attention difficulty would be diagnosed "attention-deficit/hyperactivity disorder, predominantly inattentive type." Children can also be diagnosed with "ADHD, predominantly hyperactive-impulsive type," indicating that they're hyperactive, but don't exhibit attention problems. A child exhibiting many symptoms may not merit a formal ADHD diagnosis and is labeled "attention-deficit/hyperactivity disorder not otherwise specified (NOS)."

Autism

Autism is a pervasive development disorder that may also include mental retardation or other physical disabilities. The principal signs are:

+ Difficulty understanding nonverbal behaviors, such as the ability to read facial expressions and body language
+ Inability or difficulty developing peer relationships

- Lack of empathy
- Delayed (or lack of) speech development or inability to speak
- Tendency to exhibit idiosyncratic behaviors
- Inability to play in a "make-believe" manner
- Repetitive use of language and/or repetitive motor movements
- Preoccupation with specific parts of objects
- Inflexibility in changing routines

Bipolar Disorder

Although bipolar disorder is a mood disorder cited in the DSM-IV, it is a diagnosis generally reserved for adults. Recently, however, it has become a popular practice to assign this diagnosis to children. The APA, the American Association of Child and Adolescent Psychiatrists (AACAP), and other mental health organizations believe that this disorder is rare in children. The following symptoms were not compiled from the DSM-IV, but from the various advocacy groups who subscribe to the theory that a bipolar disorder is applicable to children.

- Irritability
- Depression
- Grandiose beliefs
- Hyperactivity, inattention
- Low frustration level that easily evolves into explosive tantrums
- Aggressive behavior
- Bossy behavior
- Difficulty making a shift from one activity to another
- Night terrors
- Fear of social situations

Communication Disorders

Communication disorders are characterized by problems with the transmission and retrieval of speech. A child may have a hard time expressing herself in ways that others can understand (expressive language disorder); she may be unable to control the rate and tone of verbalizations (articulation or phonological disorder); or she may have difficulty understanding certain aspects of speech (receptive language disorder). These disorders also concern the processing of information; a person who has communication disorder may also find it hard to sort through auditory or visual stimuli.

> Communication disorders are characterized by problems with the transmission and retrieval of speech.

An auditory processing disorder may present long- or short-term memory lapses. A person may have problems following multistep instructions and separating important sounds from those that don't matter while in a noisy environment.

Those with visual processing disorders may not be able to distinguish one item from a similar one, such as determining the letter "b" from the letter "d." Delayed large motor skills can affect one's ability to run, skip, or jump. Small motor development also affects writing and other skills requiring hand-to-eye coordination.

Learning Disabilities

Learning disabilities (LD) are diagnosed by the administration of standardized achievement and intelligence tests, although LD-specific assessment inventories may also be used. When an individual is not achieving at the expected level of competence for her chronological age, intelligence (also determined by standardized tests), and expected educational levels, she would be diagnosed with a learning disability in one or more specific areas, such as reading, writing, or mathematical abilities. These deficits interfere with daily living skills and manifest themselves as visual or auditory information processing disorders.

Can't Read

Dyslexia is the term used to describe difficulty with reading accurately or with comprehension of subject matter. Dyslexia may also include the inability to spell and reversals of symbols (letters or numbers).

Can't Add

Dyscalculia is a mathematics disorder that also affects one's ability to understand abstractions. A person with dyscalculia may have a poor long-term memory for mathematical concepts. He or she may also commonly omit or reverse symbols while reading or writing math problems.

Can't Write

Dysgraphia is a writing disorder, whether it be the actual physical act or content expression. The individual may be able to complete written work, but does so very slowly in order to produce intelligible results.

Mental Retardation

Mental retardation is defined as intellectual functioning below the average IQ of 100 (determined by standardized testing). This level of impairment affects daily living skills and communication to varying degrees, depending on the severity of the disorder.

- ✦ Mild: IQ level between approximately 50 and 70
- ✦ Moderate: IQ level between approximately 35 and 55
- ✦ Severe: IQ level between approximately 20 and 40
- ✦ Profound: IQ level below 25

Oppositional Defiant Disorder (ODD)

Children with ODD, a conduct disorder, generally behave in a hostile and defiant manner toward adults. The principal signs are:

+ Loses temper

+ Deliberately annoys others

+ Blames others

+ Tends to be easily annoyed

+ Tends to be vindictive

+ Tends to be argumentative

+ Refuses to comply with rules or requests

Obsessive Compulsive Disorder (OCD)

An individual with the obsessive compulsive personality disorder has abnormal obsessions, compulsions, or both. These may include:

+ Frequent and unusual attention to washings, arranging items, touching, and continuous checking

+ Unusual fear of being contaminated by germs

+ Extreme moral concerns or religiosity, unrelated to cultural or faith-based associations

+ Developmentally inappropriate sexual or aggressive thoughts

+ Fear of harming self or others

+ Stubbornness in regard to change

+ Extreme need for perfection

+ Inability to discard broken or otherwise unusable objects

Tourette's Disorder

Tourette's is a tic disorder that produces intermittent abnormal and uncontrollable motor and verbal behaviors, such as barking, twitching, and swearing.

Other Disorders and Syndromes

Many syndromes and disorders are not accepted by the established professional medical and mental health organizations. The symptoms of these disorders frequently mirror current diagnoses with only minimal differences. The newly identified constellations of symptoms may eventually be accepted by professionals after rigorous academic research.

Nonverbal Learning Disorder (NLD)

The psychologist Helmer R. Myklebust developed the term "nonverbal learning disorder" after his research determined that many children present symptoms similar to ADHD and autism, but do not fall within the diagnostic criteria for either. They display such symptoms as:

+ Lack of motor skills and poor coordination
+ Poor visual recall
+ Inability to discern spatial relations
+ Deficits in social skills
+ Difficulty shifting from one activity to another
+ Adult-like speech and rote-reading abilities (hyperlexia) that may develop at an exceptionally early age (preschool years)
+ Excellent ability for rote memorization
+ Poor mathematics skills

Dysfunction in Sensory Integration (DSI)

Identified by occupational therapists, DSI is a cluster of symptoms similar to autism. It is often treated with physical therapies, such as hard rubbing or brushing techniques, compression of the body using weighed vests, and a special diet. Those diagnosed with this dysfunction:

+ May or may not want to be touched by others
+ May display stereotypical behaviors related to stomping, bumping, or spinning
+ May be oversensitive to sounds, tastes, odors, and clothing textures
+ May have difficulty with small and large motor skills and coordination
+ May possess processing disorders

Do these disorders actually exist? Yes, many do. Could your child be ADD or bipolar and that's why he's unable to sit still and learn? That question can only be answered by you in consultation with trusted medical and mental health professionals.

ARE TESTS AND EVALUATIONS REALLY NECESSARY?

MANY PARENTS WONDER if tests and evaluations are necessary for their child. The answer is, "It depends." Parents whose children display a clear physical disability will want standardized tests and professional evaluations. They will need formal diagnosis to qualify for such services as speech, physical, and occupational therapies through public and nonprofit providers.

Parents as Assessors

Most parents are quite capable of assessing their own child's strengths and weaknesses. Many homeschooling parents see no need to have their child's behavior or characteristics compartmentalized into little diagnostic boxes. My husband and I made the decision to seek consultations with our son's pediatrician and a clinical psychologist because we wanted to rule out mental retardation, autism, or a medical condition. Once the professionals had determined that he possessed normal intelligence and was physically healthy, we made the choice to bypass formal testing and diagnosis for potential learning disorders.

LJ, a parent in Portland, Oregon, also decided against a formal diagnosis for her homeschooled son, who has always been home-schooled. If enrolled in school, LJ's son would've been labeled because he could not read at the traditional age of eight or nine years old. Since homeschooling allowed him to learn at his own pace, he has never viewed himself as "different" for not learning to read until the age of twelve.

> Many homeschooling parents see no need to have their child's behavior or characteristics compartmentalized into little diagnostic boxes.

Parents as Researchers

Many parents decide to thoroughly research their child's "troublesome" behaviors before approaching practitioners. Many medical and mental health professionals do not appreciate parental input during the early stages of assessment. Regardless of the professionals' opinions, it's a sound practice for parents to enter the diagnostic process armed with information regarding the potential causes of your child's difficulties.

"I diagnosed my oldest son long before seeking professionals," recalls Erika, a California homeschooling mother of three sons. "It was a motherly instinct that prompted me to read about various developmental disabilities." Erika poured through Internet resources and professional research and observed other children who behaved similarly. She determined that her sons, ages three, seven, and nine, all displayed various symptoms related to autism, AS, and ADHD. The two youngest boys have never received formal diagnoses. Erika's oldest son was assessed and briefly participated in an early intervention program sponsored by the public school before the family began homeschooling.

Homeschooling parent LJ contends that diagnoses are not always necessary for a child to learn: "Adults have the power and therefore the responsibility to meet the needs of the child—with or without a label."

PROS AND CONS OF FORMAL DIAGNOSIS

YOU'RE SITTING ON the fence about seeking professional assessment. You want to do the right thing for your child, but your intuition tells you that this could be a case of a late bloomer being misdiagnosed with a serious disorder. Let's examine the positive and negative consequences of receiving a formal diagnosis for your child.

Diagnoses Can Be Helpful

On the positive side, knowing that your child has a verifiable disorder provides an understanding as to why he behaves in certain ways. Knowing that your child has difficulty sitting still or staying focused on a task will help you develop responses to work with him more effectively. Also, a diagnosis allows mental health professionals to communicate with one another using a specific term, rather than rattling off a list of symptoms each time they discuss a child's case.

Diagnoses Can Impact a Lifetime

In contrast, one of the negative side effects of a formal diagnosis is that the child may feel like "damaged goods," that he is not like other children. These children are isolated with other special needs children or pulled out of their regular classroom to participate in what most children refer to as "the dummy classes." There's a high

A HUNTER IN A FARMER'S WORLD?

The concept of ADD individuals as "hunters in a farmer's world" was popularized by Thom Hartmann, Ph.D., in his books, *Attention Deficit Disorder: A Different Perspective* and *Beyond ADD*. His theory states ADD individuals are a genetic remnant of the hunter-gatherers in early human societies. Today's hunters seek to find a way to survive in what has been a farmer's world for centuries. Thousands of years ago most people possessed hunter traits: Constantly scanning the environment for prey and danger (distractibility); quick decision-making (impulsiveness); a willingness to take risks; flexibility within time constraints (balancing between waiting for prey and actual hunting); and hyperfocusing (during the hunt). All of these are common ADD traits, which once helped the hunter societies survive and thrive. As a result, some researchers think ADD should be termed an attention "inconsistency" rather than a "deficit."

As the worldwide agricultural revolution began, followed by the more recent industrial revolution, these hunter traits became less of an advantage to the individual, as whole societies evolved from hunting for survival to farming and eventually, manufacturing. The farmer had to keep his attention focused on the tasks at hand in order to sustain a steady, dependable effort. The farmer couldn't go off wandering in the woods to check out an interesting distraction during planting time or harvest. He had to care for his animals meticulously, day in and day out, month by month, year after year. In an agricultural society, a risk-taking personality could be detrimental, but a careful, patient, and organized individual, a

likelihood these children will be teased or bullied by others, which places them at great risk for developing low self-esteem, depression, and possible suicidal ideation.

In addition, children's reactions to stressors are frequently misdiagnosed as serious mental disturbances. A child may also "act out" farmer, was likely to bring success. Stability, goal-orientation, long-range planning, and a linear sense of time (as opposed to the hunter's more flexible, elastic time-sense) are needed to assure modern survival.

Eventually hunter societies were eliminated through isolation or outright extermination. Hunters became expendable as farmers needed space and land. Today most modern cultures reward the farmer behaviors. Our schools are based on an agricultural (or industrial) model, using repetitive techniques and stressing linear rather than divergent thinking. Linear thinking is a step-by-step, organized manner of thinking. Divergent thinking involves letting things go, stepping across boundaries, and mixing ideas together in new ways. Divergent thinking is a creative style of thinking. Instead of reaching a final point, one's thoughts tend to branch out and explore. Divergent thinking is associated with the right hemisphere of the brain and linear (or convergent) thinking is associated with the left hemisphere. While divergent thinking may be compatible with creativity, linear thinking generally is associated with getting things done. Some studies have shown certain creative people are more likely to exhibit mixed or right brain dominance than the general population.

Hartmann stresses that society still needs its hunters, whether most people realize this or not. Hunters are generally the pioneers, the entrepreneurs, the agents of change, the innovators, the creators.

—KATHY WARD, EXCERPTED WITH PERMISSION FROM THE ARTICLE "UNSCHOOLING ADD," PUBLISHED IN *GENTLE SPIRIT MAGAZINE*, VOLUME 6, ISSUE 10; P.O. BOX 246, WAUNA, WA 98395. WWW.GENTLESPIRIT.COM

when suffering from a "hidden" medical condition, such as hyper- or hypothyroidism, diabetes, or some other serious illness.

Finally, if a young child has a diagnostic label affixed to her, that label may follow her throughout life. Let's say your fidgety five-year-old is driving his kindergarten teacher crazy. He peppers her with constant questions (and, of course, he doesn't raise his hand before asking them); he can't stay in his seat because he's busy exploring the classroom for "interesting stuff"; and he gets bored quickly. His teacher tells you that your son has attention-deficit/hyperactivity disorder (ADHD) and that he should be assessed and treated by a physician immediately so that he doesn't fall behind academically. Worried for your son's future, you rush him to a doctor who agrees with the ADHD diagnosis because he observed your son fidgeting impatiently (there's a great climbing tree outside the office). The doctor prescribes stimulant medication that makes your son feel crummy, but he's quiet in class and seems to be focusing better on his studies. Your son continues these medications throughout his school career and, upon graduation, decides to enlist in the military. He has a well-documented medical history of a "mental disorder" and long-term methamphetamine use. Unfortunately, the U.S. Department of Defense has a policy of rejecting recruits with such backgrounds. Although this is only one example, the potential for future abuse of medical records could prevent your child from gaining access to a long-desired career.

> The incidence of many childhood disorders would plummet by simply allowing children to mature at their own pace.

Diagnosis Is a Personal Decision

Deciding whether to seek diagnosis for your child when you recognize that his abilities differ is very much an individual decision, similar to determining whether homeschooling is the best option for your family. Many children *do benefit* from early identification and treatment. Conversely, the incidence of many childhood disorders would plummet by simply allowing children to mature at their own pace.

Whether your child is truly affected by learning difficulties or simply moves at her own unique pace, homeschooling has much to offer such a child. Families are free to experiment with various methods, materials, and learning styles. The options are endless. You move at your child's pace, using practices that emphasize his strengths and bolster his weaknesses. One of the innumerable joys of home-schooling is marveling at your child's abilities when learning finally starts to click.

SIMPLE STARTING POINTS

✦ *Read well-researched books and articles on child development.* It's helpful to understand the ages and stages theories, as well as what's considered normal and delayed development. Look for materials written by developmental or cognitive psychologists who tend to hold a "whole child" view, in contrast to educational professionals' focus on measuring learning levels. Steer clear of "trendy" ideas.

✦ *Become an "expert" on your own child.* Make a list of those behaviors you find "troublesome." Identify one or two that concern you most, then observe when those behaviors occur. Was your child tired or hungry? Has your child recently experienced a loss, such as a friend moving away or the death of a family member or beloved pet? Determining that your child was reacting to a situation outside of his control is helpful in understanding and managing difficult behaviors.

✦ *Don't rush into anything.* Becoming an expert requires time and effort. Take your time to observe your child and research possible causes for behaviors. When you think you've found your child's exact disorder, keep searching; it may not be the right one. There's no need to rush into a misdiagnosis.

✦ *Create partnerships with professionals.* Educational, medical, and mental health professionals should view parents (and the child, if appropriate) as a partner in the assessment process. These professionals must respect your input as an equal partner. If your research indicates that your child is a late bloomer and you don't agree with the practitioner's ADHD diagnosis, don't be intimidated into accepting a misdiagnosis. Find a professional who *will* work with you.

✦   *Develop an internal truth detector.* Undoubtedly, everyone has an opinion about what's "wrong" with your child and what treatment you should follow. Remember, there are no "cures." You need to wade through vast amounts of information to determine what works for you and your child. Rubber hip boots are optional.

RESOURCES

Books

Armstrong, Thomas. *The Myth of the A.D.D. Child: Fifty Ways to Improve Your Child's Behavior and Attention Span Without Drugs, Labels, or Coercion.* Plume, 1997.

Aron, Elaine N. *The Highly Sensitive Person: How to Thrive When the World Overwhelms You.* Carol Publishing, 1996.

Aron, Elaine N. *The Highly Sensitive Person's Workbook.* Broadway Books, 1999.

Breggin, Peter R. *Reclaiming Our Children: A Healing Plan for a Nation in Crisis.* Perseus Books, 2000.

Breggin, Peter R. *Talking Back to Ritalin: What Doctors Aren't Telling You About Stimulants for Children.* Common Courage Press, 1998.

Carey, William B. "Is ADHD a Valid Disorder?" Article online at www.temperament.com/WBCnihpaper.html.

Carroll, Lee, and Jan Tober (eds.). *Indigo Children: The New Kids Have Arrived.* 1999.

Green, Ross W. *The Explosive Child: A New Approach for Understanding and Parenting Easily Frustrated, "Chronically Inflexible" Children,* 2nd ed. HarperCollins, 2001.

Hartmann, Thom. *Thom Hartmann's Complete Guide to ADHD: Help for Your Family at Home, School, and Work.* Underwood Books, 2000.

Kohn, Alfie. *The Case Against Standardized Testing: Raising the Scores, Ruining the Schools.* Heinemann, 2000.

McGuinness, Diane. *When Children Don't Learn: Understanding the Biology and Psychology of Learning Disabilities.* New York: Basic Books, 1985.

Spears, Dana Scott, and Ron L. Braund. *Strong-Willed Child or Dreamer?* Thomas Nelson Publishers, 1996.

Turecki, Stanley, and Leslie Tonner. *The Difficult Child.* Bantam Books, 1985.

Virtue, Doreen. *The Care and Feeding of Indigo Children.* Hay House, 2001.

Walker III, Sydney. *A Dose of Sanity: Mind, Medicine, and Misdiagnosis.* John Wiley & Sons, 1997.

Walker III, Sydney. *The Hyperactivity Hoax: How to Stop Drugging Your Child & Find Real Medical Help.* St. Martins, 1999.

Organizations

Alliance for Childhood, P.O. Box 444, College Park, MD 20741, 301-513-1777, www.allianceforchildhood.net

American Academy of Pediatrics, 141 Northwest Point Boulevard, Elk Grove, IL 60007, 847-434-4000, www.aap.org

American Speech-Language-Hearing Association, 10801 Rockville Pike, Rockville, MD 20852, 800-638-8255 (voice or TTY), www.asha.org

Center for Study of Psychiatry & Psychology, 4628 Chestnut Street, Bethesda, MD 20814, 301-652-5580, www.breggin.com

FairTest, 342 Broadway, Cambridge, MA 02139, 607-864-4810, www.fairtest.org

Hello Friend/Ennis William Cosby Foundation, P.O. Box 4061, Santa Monica, CA 90411, www.hellofriend.org

National Center for Learning Disabilities, 381 Park Avenue South, Suite 1401, New York, NY 10016, 212-545-7510, www.ncld.org

Web Sites

Born to Explore—The Other Side of ADD: A Clearinghouse for
    Positive & Alternative Information: www.borntoexplore.com
Highly Sensitive Person Homepage: www.hsperson.com
Indigo Children: www.indigochildren.com
Nurturing Our Spirited Children: www.nurturingourfamilies.com
    /spirited/index.com

3

BUT I'M NOT A SPECIAL EDUCATION TEACHER!

In This Chapter

✦ Private schools are better, right?

✦ Developing confidence to teach your own child

✦ Renewed faith in homeschooling after returning to school

✦ Teaching is more than credentials

✦ Parents as teachers

✦ Teachers as homeschoolers

*M*OST PROSPECTIVE HOMESCHOOLING parents are concerned that they lack teaching credentials. The parent of a learning disabled or special needs child finds this especially worrisome. We're concerned that we won't be able to impart knowledge to our special children in the way a professional educator can. We witness the suffering of our children precisely within the setting designed to help them. We conclude that if trained professionals aren't able to educate our children, we as parents certainly cannot succeed. Reluctant to make the jump directly to homeschooling, many parents will try a shot at what the private sector has to offer.

PRIVATE SCHOOLS ARE BETTER, RIGHT?

TYPICALLY, IF A child struggles in a public school setting, we look to private schools, which tout smaller classrooms and specialized attention, to do a better job. In general, private schools are viewed as providing superior academics and as being more capable of meeting individual needs. But families often realize that private schools may not be better than public, so they turn to homeschooling as a last resort and are pleasantly surprised at the results.

After years of battling with religious and private schools to meet her ten-year-old son's educational needs, Lee in Massachusetts turned to homeschooling. "Last year we spent a lot of time de-schooling, plus learning what worked for my son. A lot of what we do is to provide opportunities, tutors, reading material, books on tape, and more." She reports that after a year of homeschooling, her son "is much happier and less stressed, and has more time to follow his interests." Lee says of her ADHD, dysgraphic, and gifted son, "It's also easier to meet the needs of a child whose abilities span about five grade levels." Lee does not possess a teaching credential, yet her son is thriving after one year of homeschooling.

DEVELOPING CONFIDENCE TO TEACH YOUR OWN CHILD

MAKING THE DECISION to start homeschooling is probably the most difficult step. To take this first step, you'll need to develop the confidence that you are capable of educating your own children. You need to remember that all homeschooling parents have at least once (if not more) questioned not only their qualifications to teach, but also whether they were sane to choose this radically different approach to special education.

Overcoming Doubts

One year ago, Elaine, a Texas parent, decided to remove her eight-year-old, high-functioning autistic son from school. She recalls, "I wasn't completely confident when we started homeschooling. My husband and I have always taught our son what he wanted to know as he encountered things in his life. It seemed that homeschooling would be just a little more than we've always done. Upon discovering the wealth of materials available, I felt I could do fine." Elaine's concerns about her son's education extended beyond wondering about her own ability to teach him. "The people with 'teaching credentials' were not doing a good job of reaching my son or trying to understand how he learned in a classroom with more than seven students. I often had to explain his autism to his teachers, and I felt it wasted a good part of our day."

> To take the first step toward homeschooling, you need to develop the confidence that you are capable of educating your own children.

A homeschooling friend advised Beryl, a parent in Michigan, to remove her special needs daughter from school. "My first thought was, 'There is no way I could educate my own child. I need to leave that to the 'professionals,' yet my friend responded that because I know my child better than anyone, I would do a wonderful job." Four years after making the decision, Beryl now states, "I find myself echoing these same words to newcomers considering homeschooling."

Bolstering Confidence with Research

Linda, a parent in southern California whose son is dyslexic, remembers reaching her decision to homeschool by balancing her own doubts with what she had discovered in her researches. "Initially, I wasn't confident at all. My son had real needs; I wanted him to receive the best education possible, yet I was very concerned I wouldn't be able to provide that. It was intimidating to hear numerous teachers say that they wouldn't even consider teaching their own children outside of a classroom setting." This negative response notwithstanding, Linda wasn't easily dissuaded and continued to seek more information. "I surveyed specialists and anyone who could possibly have any kind of opinion: several psychologists and medical doctors, more than half a dozen accredited teachers, friends who worked with special needs kids. Based on what they told me, I decided I couldn't do any worse than what he was already receiving in school. The school's process wasn't specialized in addressing my son's needs, and he wasn't benefiting from being in an inflexible teaching environment. I was distressed at how limited training is for school officials."

Linda started tutoring her son after school: "It was very illuminating to hear teachers define their day's value as being only what material was covered (of course, much of this was with parents doing homework in the evenings)." She recalls an eye-opening experience: "I read how forty-five minutes of one-on-one tutoring could equal a day's worth of teaching." They've been homeschooling for four years and haven't looked back. "It's so easy," she adds, "because now we work during my son's 'best hours' rather than supplementing after a long school day."

Since starting to homeschool, Linda has discovered in herself a renewed interest in learning and has returned to college to pursue graduate studies in psychology. What she's learning in her studies is solidifying her belief that a homeschooling parent can be superior to a credentialed teacher. Linda states, "One of my professors specializes in the study of creativity. Her dozen or more studies indicated that creativity in second grade children was greatly diminished by sixth grade. My professor felt this was due to children spending hours in school classrooms that aren't appropriate for them. This, along with my informal teacher surveys, supports my belief. Creativity is stifled in those individuals who endure the credentialing process."

RENEWED FAITH IN HOMESCHOOLING AFTER RETURNING TO SCHOOL

FOR MANY OF US, it's difficult to relinquish the notion that children can learn only in a classroom. Some homeschooling parents have lost confidence and returned their children to school, only to bring them right back home.

"At times, my confidence wavered, and my children went to public school for short periods," recalls Louise, a Utah parent whose ten children have varying special needs. "But in school, they always regressed, losing all the skills they learned at home. But seeing this has helped me feel more competent as a teacher. My children may not ever learn as much as 'normal' children, but they're learning all the time while at home, and this is much more than they've ever accomplished in public school."

> For many of us, it's difficult to relinquish the notion that children can learn only in a classroom.

TEACHING IS MORE THAN CREDENTIALS

LET'S EXAMINE WHAT makes a "good teacher." Would you qualify as a good teacher? Many education experts acknowledge that just because a person earns a teaching credential does not automatically mean that he or she gains the qualities needed to be a successful teacher. The National Education Association (NEA) sponsors an on-line symposium for student teachers that taps the insights of veteran educators. One such professional, Sandra Lee Jones, Ed.D., associate professor of education at Troy State University, stated:

Teaching is more than the sum of the knowledge acquired in a teacher education program. Teaching also requires excellent interpersonal skills, common sense, quick thinking, the ability to use a wide range of information sources to make the best decision, the ability to communicate in a variety of situations effectively, and many other skills not measured by a standardized test.

> "Teaching is more than the sum of the knowledge acquired in a teacher education program."

Homeschooling parent Julia of New York agrees that much more goes into becoming a teacher than merely getting the proper credentials. She views teacher training as an easier alternative to more rigorous academic pursuits. "I attended a college with a teacher training program. Witnessing the training of teachers is like watching people make hot dogs—you never look at the end product the same way after seeing how the job was handled. What caught my attention was watching student after student fail out of the academic programs or other colleges, only to enter the teaching program. To me," Julia sadly concludes, "it seemed that the teachers of the nation would be made up largely by those who could not or would not finish another academic major."

Good Teacher Qualities

A survey of online occupational guidelines, university teacher training standards, and statements of veteran teachers yielded the following list of the qualities and skills crucial for those interested in teaching:

- ✦ Patience
- ✦ Flexibility and openness to change
- ✦ The ability to see the interrelatedness of all subjects
- ✦ Being a generally well-balanced individual
- ✦ The ability to take care of oneself (physically and mentally)

- ✦ A tendency to be reflective
- ✦ The desire to make a difference in the lives of special needs children
- ✦ The ability to adapt and develop materials to suit each child's special needs
- ✦ The capacity to assist children in developing emotionally, including the facility for learning acceptable social behaviors, acquiring comfort in social situations, and preparing for life as an adult
- ✦ The ability to solve problems

PARENTS AS TEACHERS

DON'T YOU, AS a parent, already use many teaching skills daily? True, you may not possess the certification, but to homeschool your own child, you have all the necessary skills, plus one additional component—love.

There are no state mandates requiring special needs children to be taught by only credentialed special education teachers. Since you're not going to be teaching children other than your own, a credential is not required. You won't be required to enroll in college pedagogy or classroom management courses. There's no teachers' union to join, although you might decide to connect with a state or national homeschooling organization.

Instead, as a homeschooling teacher, you will be learning more about how your child processes information and how to encourage her strengths, while at the same time developing methods to overcome her weaknesses and determining how she reacts to various environmental factors related to her learning styles and abilities.

As a homeschooling teacher, you will lead your children on explorations far beyond where they'd go in a classroom. You will have

As a homeschooling teacher, you will lead your children on explorations far beyond where they'd go in a classroom.

the freedom to tailor learning experiences to each child's individual needs and interests. You will discover talents that neither you nor any teacher ever thought your child could possibly have.

The late Mark Van Doren, American poet, critic, and English professor at Columbia University, once stated: "The art of teaching is the art of assisting discovery." Let this be your maxim whenever you question your ability to teach your child.

TEACHERS AS HOMESCHOOLERS

CERTIFIED TEACHERS ARE among the many of those who have chosen to join the ranks of homeschoolers; they've chosen to abandon their teaching careers or put them on hold while homeschooling their own children.

Susan, who was a teacher in Louisiana, declares, "I became an educator because I didn't like the way things are done in schools, and I wanted to help bring about change. However, my priorities changed once my own daughter came along. I realized that changing the world needed to start with her." Susan and her husband have always homeschooled their gifted and dyslexic daughter, who is now seven years old.

Evelyn, a special education teacher in Alabama, decided to homeschool her four adopted special needs children precisely because she knew she could provide for them better through homeschooling. "I'm appalled at the lack of education my kids have gotten in special education classes. At times I've been so enthused while working on a unit study for my class and wished my own children's teachers would do something like this. I finally decided to become their teacher to do those things with them. I've taught in three districts, my kids have attended schools in four districts, and I've learned that special education programs generally do not teach to the child's fullest potential."

Parents from all walks of life and with varying educational levels are homeschooling their children whose abilities differ from the norm. Many simply cannot find any aspect of the classroom setting meeting their children's needs. These parents, regardless of individual teaching qualifications, are educating their children successfully.

SIMPLE STARTING POINTS

✦ *Read a few books on teaching methods.* You'll soon realize that teacher training is intended for the masses, not for homeschooling one's own child. These books can be checked out of the library (you may need to request an interlibrary transfer from a college library) or purchased inexpensively at yard sales and thrift shops.

✦ *Make a list of your strengths and talents.* Cast aside any notions of modesty to examine those qualities that make you great teacher material for your child. Keep in mind that it's humanly impossible to be patient, flexible, or maintain any other nurturing traits with everyone at all times.

✦ *Read homeschooling books and periodicals.* There are numerous books available in libraries and retail bookstores. Some are biographical; others are more inspirational or how-to manuals. Subscribe to a homeschooling publication for bimonthly encouragement.

✦ *Connect with others in your profession.* Professionals in every field need to network among themselves, and homeschooling parents are no different. Locate support groups in your region, subscribe to e-mail lists, or visit online chat rooms to avail yourself the opportunity to brainstorm ideas with other like-minded professionals.

I LEFT TEACHING TO HOMESCHOOL MY OWN CHILD

Sadly, many enter teaching professions for the wrong reasons; they're there for the days off and not to educate our future. I went into the field to educate and that is what I did for twenty years. During the two decades that I taught in the public school system, I saw the home lives of children and parental support change for the worse. When I began teaching, I had all the support needed; if a child had a problem, parents would listen to my concerns, and blame for the problem wasn't assigned. As this changed through the years, parents blamed me for their children's discipline problems, and at times, my life was threatened. Still, I felt these children deserved an education, and I did my best. For a few years, I taught special education classes, which was sad because many of the children didn't need to be in a learning- or behavior-disordered class. Many were in the classes simply because their attendance brought government funding to the schools. It was such an injustice to the children that I felt I really was not making a difference anymore.

Teaching in private schools wasn't as heart-rending. But the administration expected children to fit into a cookie-cutter mold, and if they didn't, it was made

RESOURCES

Books

Cohen, Cafi. *Homeschooling: The Teen Years.* Prima Publishing, 2000.

Colfax, David, and Micki Colfax. *Hard Times in Paradise: An American Family's Struggle to Carve Out a Homestead in California's Redwood Mountains.* Warner, 1992.

clear that they didn't belong in the school. Since I taught from the perspective that each child learns differently, I also didn't belong at such a school.

When my own son was involved in a serious accident and suffered traumatic brain injury, I examined our educational options. He certainly didn't fit a cookie-cutter mold, so private schools were out of the question. Public schools weren't even considered because I knew he'd be thrown into a class with children who did not suffer similar problems, thus his needs wouldn't be met.

I was concerned that he would become socially deprived if we home-schooled. However, we now realize that he has so much socialization with other homeschoolers, it sometimes seemed like we have a hard time fitting in the schoolwork!

My child is being better educated at home than in any school setting. I firmly believe each child learns differently and should have the right to do so. Too many parents just accept what's happening in schools today.

I've experienced the classroom, watched the changes, and if I had younger children, I would choose homeschooling for them from the start.

—JILL, A FORMER TEACHER IN THE LOUISIANA PUBLIC SCHOOLS

Colfax, David, and Micki Colfax. *Homeschooling for Excellence: How to Take Charge of Your Child's Education—And Why You Absolutely Must.* Warner, 1988.

Dobson, Linda. *Homeschooling: The Early Years.* Prima Publishing, 1999.

Guterson, David. *Family Matters: Why Homeschooling Makes Sense.* Harcourt Brace, 1992.

Henry, Shari. *Homeschooling: The Middle Years.* Prima Publishing, 2000.

Holt, John Caldwell. *Learning All the Time.* Addison-Wesley, 1989.

Leistico, Agnes. *I Learn Better by Teaching Myself and Still Teaching Ourselves: And, Still Teaching Ourselves.* Holt Associates, 1987. (This book, unfortunately, is out of print, but may be available in libraries or used book outlets.)

Nagel, Greta. *The Tao of Parenting: The Ageless Wisdom of Taoism and the Art of Raising Children.* Penguin, 1998.

Nagel, Greta. *The Tao of Teaching: The Special Meaning of the Tao Te Ching as Related to the Art and Pleasures of Teaching.* Donald I. Fine, 1994.

Wallace, Nancy. *Better Than School: One Family's Declaration of Independence.* Holt Associates, 1983. (This book, unfortunately, is out of print, but may be available in libraries or used book outlets.)

4

REMOVING YOUR CHILD
FROM SCHOOL

In This Chapter

+ The blame game

+ Reasons for leaving school

+ Leaving the system

*Y*OU'VE REACHED THE end of your rope with organized education. Your child, once joyfully bursting with inquisitiveness, has mutated into a sullen, despondent drone. His teacher has referred to him using such phrases as "learning disabled" and "difficulty staying on task." Teachers and school counselors have warned you that early intervention is necessary. Otherwise, if your child doesn't learn to color within the lines by age five, he could suffer long-lasting academic repercussions that may block his entrance to an Ivy League college. Although your intuitive parental voice tells you this notion is ridiculous, you still worry about your child's well-being and ability to learn.

Far too often, parents follow the advice of well-meaning educational or mental health experts, only to realize years later that despite the early interventions, the child has still fallen between the cracks in the education system. All those years spent struggling with the child, all of the money spent, and for naught. More families are taking charge of their lives by telling the schools, "As a parent I know what is best for my child, and this setting no longer meets our needs. We'll be moving on, thank you very much."

THE BLAME GAME

THE "BLAME GAME" explains much of our dissatisfaction with traditional schooling for special needs children. The teachers, administrators, and other professionals blame the child and the parents; the parents blame the educators and mental health professionals, while wondering how much could actually be the child's fault. Who does the child blame? Himself.

> You must try to resist the temptation to blame an inattentive child for not buckling down to improve his grades.

Whatever the ages of their children, parents need to realize that these children are going to blame themselves for school and social failures. You must try to resist the temptation to blame an inattentive child for not buckling down to improve his grades. Nor should you mete out punishment for public meltdowns. In the early school years, when problems first become evident, your child will simply not possess the tools to sort through her inattentiveness or emotional reactions. Teachers and parents, the key adults in a child's life, are the ones ultimately responsible for helping her get through difficult learning and social situations. Yet at the same time, those adults typically blame one another rather than acting as advocates for the child. One side needs to take control from the other to do what is best for the child. You should not find this a difficult choice because you have greater love for your child than does any education system, and you have a stake in her future. If you're still thinking that professionals are better equipped to assess and deal with your child's learning needs, read on to obtain insight about how your child's difficulties are perceived by the educational establishment designed to help them.

Galen Alessi, Ph.D., a psychology professor at Western Michigan University, conducted a study of fifty school psychologists in the United States, each of whom had an average caseload of one hundred children with learning or behavioral problems. Alessi asked the school psychologists to review and identify what they deemed the primary factors that prevented their students from learning. Alessi asked them to assign the factors to five general areas:

1. Curriculum did not meet the needs of the child.

2. The teacher was not properly implementing the curriculum.

3. The principals and school administrators lacked appropriate management skills.

4. The parents were not providing sufficient at-home learning support.

5. The child suffered from a physiological or psychology disorder.

None of these school psychologists, who served approximately five thousand students, cited the school-related factors as hindering a child's ability to learn. Rather, the notion of uninvolved parents and problem students were what all professionals surveyed blamed when a child wasn't learning. This small sample of professionals never even considered that poor staffing and practices or a possible mismatch between curriculum and child could impair learning. Do you still feel that those educational professionals who blame others rather than seek solutions are your child's best advocates?

REASONS FOR LEAVING SCHOOL

IF YOU DO not see professionals as being your child's best advocate, you are not alone, although the reasons you choose to act on this belief and homeschool may not be the same as those of other families. Homeschooling families express varied reasons for removing their children from school, ranging from school safety to better academics, with many other factors in between. Families of learning disabled and other special children cite similar concerns, but also confront an entirely different subset of needs. High on the list of reasons for opting out of public education is that parents are simply tired of fighting for federally mandated services. Realizing that a child may be experiencing learning difficulties, parents and teachers may request assistance from school counselors and psychologists. However, caseloads are large, assessment time is limited, and many children's learning differences are improperly identified. Untold numbers of children are found to possess difficulties, but are not sufficiently impaired to fall within the guidelines for school assistance.

Children who experience difficulties learning are also at risk for developing depression and anxiety because they feel they aren't as "smart" as other children. ADD and autistic spectrum children have the added misery of sensory overload within the chaotic confines of the classroom. On the playground, these children feel equally inferior because their social skills are awkward, inappropriate, or just plain goofy.

Parents have varied reasons for abandoning traditional schooling for their differently abled children. Collectively, however, there is one prevailing impetus—their children have been abandoned by traditional education.

The Battle for Special Services

School officials will tantalize parents by dangling special services such as small classes and free therapies. These services may help, but the child will need them throughout his education. Instead of recognizing this, when the child progresses under the classroom modifications, the school deems the child "cured" and removes the services, leaving the child to resume the struggle to learn.

Carole, a parent in Massachusetts, states, "My son's school didn't want to continue services for him. We were informed that since Michael was doing so well, his classroom accommodations would be eliminated. He was able to do so well precisely because of the assistance. Bottom line—we live in a town where education beyond high school isn't encouraged, and we want our son to strive for a better education. I'd rather spend my time with my kids than fighting for services I can provide myself."

Linda, a southern California mother, recalls that "my son's second grade teacher caught a sight problem that was successfully treated with great results. He began learning so easily that I figured going back and reviewing a few key concepts would be tremendously helpful for him. The school officials disagreed. I was told they were not equipped to go back and review what he had already covered in his special education class. Their special needs program was not designed to review previously learned concepts; there was no built-in flexibility. Rather than allow my son to lose quality learning time, I followed the school's advice and began tutoring him myself. It was a huge step for me because in my community, educators and parents felt that we aren't capable of teaching our own kids."

Lack of Services

In other cases, schools realize the programs need improvement, but they expect parents to accept the substandard services as better than none at all. Jennifer, a mother in California, remembers, "The school did not have the resources that would work for our son, and they admitted it. But they felt what they were providing was 'good enough.' We felt he wasn't progressing at all, if anything, he was learning a lot of bad behaviors in school." On her decision to home-school her eight-year-old epileptic/mild cerebral palsied son, Jennifer says, "When I saw the upcoming year's placement options for my son, I decided I was tired of fighting the school district for services he was never going to get. We found a Brain Gym class that helped him more than anything the school did. I realized I could do more for him at home."

Misidentification or No Identification of Disabilities

Many children have multiple traits that prevent them from learning. Although the fields of psychology and education provide generic diagnostic criteria, very rarely does a child fit perfectly into such perimeters. Rather, a child may possess a couple of ADD traits, a little bit of Asperger's Syndrome, a pinch of sensory dysfunction, but no single concrete diagnosis. Without a diagnosis, schools cannot provide special education services. Some children may never exhibit enough symptoms for a diagnosis and are left to languish in mainstream classrooms.

"Schools talk a lot about helping children with special needs," says Susan in Louisiana, "but I doubt my daughter would have been identified in a regular school system. Her giftedness hides her dyslexia, making it difficult to accurately diagnose. Conversely, her dyslexia makes her seem less intelligent since her skills lag so far behind her comprehension."

Lee, the Massachusetts parent whose gifted son also has ADHD and dysgraphia, encountered similar difficulties when her son was ten. "He'd skipped second grade and was in a mixed third-fourth grade classroom at a Jewish day school. He couldn't learn Hebrew, which was interfering with his reading and writing. Other subjects were at his reading level, but not at his thinking/discussion level. Science was also too easy, but at least he enjoyed it. We realized he couldn't stay in this program, so we looked to private schools. Unfortunately, this wasn't much better," she recalls. "Of all the private schools we considered, the one that seemed a good fit for my son decided it didn't want to deal with his dysgraphia. The school also felt he had major gaps in math. He didn't realize that a sheet of math problems he'd been given when we visited the private school was a placement test, and he didn't complete it. I'd say most private schools aren't prepared to deal with special needs."

Lee decided to examine the local public school's options because "I'm paying exorbitant property taxes to live in a suburb with a supposedly excellent school system." There, she met with the special education team whose members wanted her son to repeat third grade so that he'd again be with children his own age. Frustrated, she pointed out that her son had been achieving at or above grade level in a combined third/fourth-grade class where his primary problem had been in Hebrew, which was not taught in the public school. Lee recalls, "His main problem in the public setting appeared only to be his writing, which could be assisted with occupational therapy accommodations. It finally dawned on me that the public school didn't want him in the fourth grade because Massachusetts has high-stakes testing at this level, and a dysgraphic fourth grader would hurt their scores. Needless to say, I left that meeting vowing my son would never darken the doors of that school. Unfortunately, through all of this, my son became clinically depressed."

> Some children may never exhibit enough symptoms for a diagnosis and are left to languish in mainstream classrooms.

School-Induced Emotional Problems

"Different" children have a greater risk of developing depressive and anxiety disorders. Cindy, a California parent, remembers her Down's Syndrome/autistic son's days in a public preschool early intervention program. "He'd always be extremely stressed, overstimulated, and anxious in the classroom environment. The school wasn't willing to change in order to accommodate his needs or learning style."

Children often look to other means to stop the emotional pain. A northern California mother, Linda, recalls the days when school would call her to pick up her daughter early for what was deemed bad behavior. "She'd get so upset that she'd threaten to kill herself and her teachers; all while she was only seven. Eventually the school counselor suggested I place my daughter in a mental hospital because the bad fits didn't end." Shortly after removing her daughter from school, Linda discovered the reasons behind her daughter's reactions when a child psychiatrist recognized her behavior as Asperger's Syndrome. They've been happily home-schooling for years.

> "She'd get so upset that she'd threaten to kill herself and her teachers; all while she was only seven."

The painful memories still haunt Rhonda in Michigan. "School stress was listed as part of my son's official diagnosis," she says. "Everyone except school officials agreed the frustration and stress from school made him worse. He was fine in the summer months, so it didn't take a genius to figure out school was the problem." The stress was more than Rhonda's son could handle. "He had suicidal ideation for the better part of two years and did make an attempt to take his life," she says. "We were fortunate that his counselor was a homeschooler and suggested we remove him from school. We believe it saved his life! Now that he's in his second year of homeschooling, he has had zero suicidal ideation."

Lisa, in Michigan, recalls the struggle with her fifteen-year-old daughter's school and teacher. "The school program was a mess. The teacher was burned out and could not be held accountable, and she blamed me for all of my child's problems." Lisa's daughter has autism with mental impairment, gross motor delay, and epilepsy, yet the school seemed to disregard the seriousness of her needs. "My daughter had anxiety attacks getting off the bus each day, which was bad enough, then her health deteriorated," Lisa says. "She was seriously underweight because they could not or would not feed her all day. Finally, the teacher decided my child's diagnosis should be changed to a degenerative disorder, even after our doctor stated that this was impossible. The teacher refused to accept the doctor's determination and continued to write reports that supported her belief. I felt this provided an excuse for the teacher since she had no expectations my daughter would make any progress. I don't think she wanted my daughter to succeed because it would prove the teacher wrong. There were no other appropriate options for a teacher or classroom, so we decided to homeschool." Lisa has been homeschooling her daughter for six years.

Sensory Overload

Many special needs children are made miserable by environmental stimuli such as constant classroom chatter, fluorescent overhead lighting, or the rattling of chairs and desks.

"My daughter is sound sensitive," says Tammy in Alaska of her eleven-year-old autistic daughter. "Regardless of whether Pamela ended up in a special education (likely) or mainstream classroom, she would fight the barrage of noise inevitable in most school settings. It's one thing learning to cope with noisy settings, which she has, but it's another to be forced to learn complex skills in that setting!"

Tammy also felt she could better address her daughter's needs through homeschooling. "When she was in school, I spent ten hours a week supplementing. I was the one teaching her, then informing the disbelieving teacher 'Pamela can do X.' Then I'd have to show them how I taught her. It slowly dawned on me," she says, "that school was a waste of time. My daughter needed one-to-one teaching, which is hard to find in the school system. Further, every time she had a new teacher, valuable time was lost as the teacher tried to figure out how Pamela learns best (if the teacher even bothered). By homeschooling her, I provide continuity from year to year!"

Linda remembers the consequences her daughter suffered while enrolled in school. "The special education school overstimulated my daughter. The school bus ride bothered her, as did the crowds of people, the physical education activities in the gym, and the excessive rules and restrictions placed on her. She often was removed from class due to bad behavior brought on by her overstimulation, and placed in the 'support room,' which was essentially solitary confinement. She was restrained to the floor by a school employee sitting on her until she would agree to cooperate."

Social Misfit

Special needs children very often have difficulty socializing with peers. The special child may be delayed in developing appropriate social skills or may display somewhat odd or "clueless" behaviors. Other children simply experience a sensory overload in typical play settings and tend to isolate themselves.

Dawn in Wisconsin recalls the difficulty her son had in elementary school. Although her son had not been diagnosed with any disorder, it was apparent to Dawn that he was somehow socially "different." She looked forward to her son's future beyond elementary school, hopeful that he would be socially accepted. "We enrolled him in junior high, hoping that he would fit in. It didn't happen. Our son received death threats during school, and he was abused by other students. Junior high is a nightmare for someone like my son." Dawn's son was not succeeding academically either. "When my husband and I attended the parent-teacher meetings in March, all seven of our son's teachers told us the same thing. 'He's lost and has no idea what is going on around him,'" she says. "By the time we talked with the last teacher, we just wanted to get our son through the year. We told the teacher we were going to homeschool him the following year, and the teacher said it would be the best thing we could possibly do." Dawn's son was eventually diagnosed with Asperger's Syndrome.

Elaine, a Texas mother of an eight-year-old high-functioning autistic son, decided to homeschool because her son's schooling prevented him from enjoying the real world. "My son was tired and unwilling to pursue other interests after a long day of sitting still at school. He often seemed to be 'in another world' at lunchtime and didn't socialize much with others. I felt my son was missing enjoyable experiences because he was so often burdened with 'busy work' assignments. I truly enjoy my son's company and missed doing many things together!"

Homeschooling Just Works for Us

Most families have multiple and broader reasons for turning to homeschooling. Although their child's special needs were the primary reason for homeschooling, many parents have experienced several disappointments with traditional schooling.

"Our children were only enrolled in school for a very short time, but it didn't take long to come up with reasons to homeschool," Jill in California reflects. "There were serious discipline problems at school (not with our children but with others at school), we were dissatisfied with the curriculum and unhappy with the overall social and educational climate at the school." Moreover, Jill missed the family closeness and the flexible autonomy of having her children at home. Finally, she didn't like the one-size-fits-all system of teaching. Jill emphatically states, "Our children's individual needs were not being met, on any level."

LJ in Oregon found the quality of teachers to be a particular problem. "Despite the fact that many of my friends are teachers, I find the majority of them to be, well, a nice word is clueless. Homeschooling is easier than trying to identify the few good teachers each year." Besides, she adds, "My parenting style is designed for special needs."

Some families initially consider homeschooling for safety reasons, only to later realize the numerous benefits. Lesa in California is one such parent. "I had thought of homeschooling for about a year, but my original reasons were more for safety, morality, and drugs. Even though we live in a very affluent area, I was afraid of what I saw on the news about public schools." Then, additional reasons started to pile up. "When my son was in sixth grade I became more disturbed by what I saw in his middle school. Kids were crammed into classrooms, sometimes as many as forty-two; the teachers were exhausted and unprepared to deal with anyone other than a completely simple kid. My son was placed in honors classes, but wasn't helped with his special needs."

> "Homeschooling is easier than trying to identify the few good teachers each year."

Lesa's twelve-year-old son has difficulties with inattention and writing and has no visual depth perception. Although writing assignments remained arduous for him, he was nevertheless able to complete them using a computer, but the school wouldn't allow this accommodation. "He was completely frustrated and no one was noticing!" exclaims Lesa. "Finally with a lot of support from a local homeschooling e-mail group, I pulled my son out of school midyear. He needs to be challenged yet accommodated at the same time, I can do that!"

Individual attention makes all the difference between success and failure for many children. Kathy in northern California says of her fourteen-year-old ADHD son, "In the school setting, everything just went over his head. Now he gets the one-on-one attention he needs. He understands more, has more self-confidence, and now he has the desire to learn!" Kathy and her son have also discovered other benefits of homeschooling: "He was always in trouble in the classroom, and we were unable to work with the teacher to make the situation better." She adds, "Now, he just loves being out in the community! We belong to a support group and participate in many field trips."

For many parents, the realization that their child is not progressing academically is a key incentive for homeschooling. After all, could a parent do any worse than the school? "After our son was diagnosed with Asperger's Syndrome by a psychologist, I quit my job one day and removed him from school the next," recalls Dawn in Wisconsin of the swiftness of events five years ago. "We used the Alpha Omega testing service to assess where he was academically, and the results floored me! We tried again using a different program only to receive the same sad results. Our son's scores indicated his academic skills were at first and second grade levels, yet he'd passed from grade to grade in public school!" She continues, "We believe he stopped learning in the second grade when he started taking Ritalin, which caused him to be 'stoned.' So, at age thirteen, we started with the basics because he had no academic foundation to build upon. The advantage we had was his age, which provided him with a greater ability to understand at an increased rate." Dawn's son was finally able to grasp academics. "We started using the Alpha Omega Lifepacs series to fill in the gaps. We continued with projects through the summer because in our book, everyday is a day to learn." She proudly cites her son's progress. "He's now working at grade level and even a grade above in biology. Homeschooling has been a blessing far beyond anything we could've imagined. It's not always been easy, but the rewards are tremendous."

LEAVING THE SYSTEM

NOW THAT YOU'VE decided to homeschool, your next step is removing your child from the school. Homeschooling is a legal and viable educational option in all fifty states. Unfortunately, many individuals and educational institutions do not realize this and frequently tell families who ask about homeschooling that it's illegal. It is not. Some states don't have specific homeschooling laws; this doesn't mean, however, that home education is illegal. In most states, there are generally a few options for educating your child at home legally, such as through private school independent study programs or declaring your home a private school. Many school personnel either aren't aware of such options or choose not to provide the information. And although educating others about the legality of homeschooling is certainly a noble and important cause to champion, your main concern in this early stage is to focus on removing your child from school in the most expedient manner that causes the least angst.

The laws vary with each state, so be sure to check with your state homeschooling organization or a local support group for specific details on your legal options. National homeschooling organizations are the best place to start; they can point you toward the laws and direct you to other helpful organizations.

Wherever you are, you're best off not giving numerous details about why you are removing your child from school. You want your departure to be as amiable as possible.

What if you have already blown off steam and told the school principal that you plan to homeschool? Have you done irreparable harm? Probably not. If, when you inform the school that you're removing your child, officials ask you whether you still plan to homeschool, simply reply that you've reconsidered and plan to examine all options from private schools to homeschooling, and thank them for their concern. In these cases, the school staff does not need to know that the "school" is actually in your home. Another useful (and truthful) response is: "We have found a private school that will better meet our child's needs. The school does offer an independent study program that is an option we intend to investigate further."

Your child is out of school; you're officially among the ranks of homeschoolers. Now what? Let's examine how you can best address your child's needs through his or her unique learning styles and the various methods of homeschooling available.

SIMPLE STARTING POINTS

✦ *Know your state's laws!* This is the first thing you must do before removing your child from school. Otherwise you might be cited for truancy. National organizations can direct you to state home-schooling organizations. Many state organizations have county contacts or listings of regional support groups that offer further assistance. Familiarize yourself with your state legal options and specific county practices.

✦ *Make lists of all the things you and your special child would like to do and learn while homeschooling.* There are a couple of ways to approach this task. You and your child can write a list together; or you can each write separate lists and compare them over a leisurely snack. This list can then be used as an outline for your homeschooling studies!

✦ *Take time to rediscover family life.* Families with a special needs child frequently have time for little else. After removing your child from school, spend time each day to do something fun and special together, like a family story time, song, prayer, or meal. See chapter 7 for more ideas.

RESOURCES

Web Sites

About.com's Homeschooling Website: www.homeschooling.about
    .com/education/homeschooling
A to Z Home's Cool: www.gomilpitas.com/homeschooling
Jon's Homeschool Resource Page: www.midnightbeach.com/hs
Homeschool.com: www.homeschool.com
Homeschool Zone: www.homeschoolzone.com

5

WORKING WITH YOUR UNIQUE CHILD

In This Chapter

✦ Multiple intelligences

✦ Turning learning theories into homeschooling practices

ONE OF THE reasons many of us educate our children at home is because they've either been identified as having learning disabilities or as being "at risk" for developing them. This label generally means nothing more than a child learns differently from the methods that most schools use to teach. Keeping a child in the rigid school setting will lead to a declining sense of self-worth and the onset of "learned helplessness." This condition develops when a person feels helpless to succeed in situations (e.g., school work and social relationships), thus expecting failures as an accepted way of life.

If a child is constantly reminded that she's not as smart or capable as other children, she eventually stops trying to succeed.

As society has evolved, its members have become less tolerant of individual differences. Where it was once acceptable to be skilled in one or two areas, more emphasis is now placed on individual successes across all disciplines. The individual who was once deemed a master in a field is now viewed as a burden on the system for not being equipped to perform multiple duties along numerous disciplines. Countering this view, however, is a research-based theory that there is not one single entity, "intelligence"; rather, there are multiple "intelligences," for example, musical, spatial, verbal, and the like. The theory of multiple intelligences casts aside the notions that to be "intelligent" one must possess talents across the academic spectrum and again makes it acceptable to be good in only a few specific areas.

MULTIPLE INTELLIGENCES

BASED ON RESEARCH findings within the fields of neuroscience, anthropology, and history, Harvard psychologist Howard Gardner has proposed that we all have varying degrees of multiple intelligences, not only the linguistic and mathematical styles that schools typically use in their curricula. Initially Gardner cited seven intelligences, then added an eighth in 1996. Although not everyone agrees with Gardner's thoughts on intelligence, his theories have proved useful to many homeschoolers.

Gardner's Eight Multiple Intelligences

1. Visual/Spatial Intelligence
   + Thinks and learns from images such as movies and photographs
   + Engages in art projects
   + Uses maps and graphs with ease

- Enjoys puzzles and mazes
- Spends a lot of time daydreaming

2. Verbal/Linguistic Intelligence
   - Is sensitive to words and their meanings
   - Enjoys writing
   - Is a natural storyteller
   - Spells well

3. Musical Intelligence
   - Understands and creates music
   - Possesses a perfect pitch for musical tones
   - Listens to music while studying
   - Enjoys listening to music

4. Kinesthetic Intelligence
   - Uses body for expression or to attain goals
   - Fidgets a lot when seated
   - Enjoys participating in sports
   - Touches others when conversing

5. Logical/Mathematical Intelligence
   - Understands complex logical systems
   - Can quickly compute problems mentally
   - Enjoys computers
   - Shows keen reasoning abilities

6. Interpersonal Intelligence
   - Understands other people
   - Socializes effortlessly
   - Prefers group activities
   - Acts as mediator to settle others' disputes

7. Intrapersonal Intelligence

    ✦ Understands the inner workings of own emotions

    ✦ Is strong-willed and independent

    ✦ Prefers solitary activities

    ✦ Is self-motivated

8. Naturalist Intelligence

    ✦ Understands patterns in a natural environment

    ✦ Collects natural objects and data such as shells, leaves, and birds' nests

    ✦ Uses magnifiers, microscopes, telescopes, and binoculars

    ✦ Enjoys activities related to nature such as hiking, gardening, caring for animals, and participating in wildlife protection projects

Psychologist and former learning disabilities specialist Thomas Armstrong has demystified Gardner's academic model into a practical one useful for parents and teachers who want to incorporate this theory into their work with children. After years of working with special education children in both public and private schools, Armstrong became convinced that the notion of learning disabilities allowed the educational system to divert blame away from itself and onto alleged brain disorders of children. Armstrong felt that children not achieving in school was due to differences in learning styles, rather than an invisible handicap. Armstrong left the education profession to conduct research into alternatives to the current school system and now advocates for addressing learning *differences* as opposed to the disability model.

Both Gardner and Armstrong strongly caution against identifying a child as possessing only one or two of the intelligences, while ignoring the full spectrum. Using multiple intelligences isn't meant to increase your child's IQ scores. Rather, you should view the theory as a tool that allows you to better understand the various ways your child learns. Some children possess strengths in numerous intelligences; others fit perfectly into only one. Use what works best with your child while maintaining a flexible understanding that children have the capacity to change very quickly; what works well today may not be appropriate in a month.

It's also important to provide your child with a variety of opportunities and tools with which to develop experimentally their innate intelligences.

The veteran educator Laurel Schmidt recalls her own childhood filled with opportunities to explore and a ready supply of simple materials (paper, pencils, tools, and books) to start her on her journey. Most important, she had inquisitive and encouraging parents who enjoyed discovery as much as their children did. She states in her book, *Seven Times Smarter,* "The more life in my classroom felt like my childhood, the smarter my kids were. Over the years, I learned to spot intelligence at fifty paces and coax it out of kids convinced that they were dumb."

> Some children possess strengths in numerous intelligences; others fit perfectly into only one.

TURNING LEARNING THEORIES INTO HOME-SCHOOLING PRACTICES

HOW MANY OF these traits do you see in your child? Many? A few? Use your child's intelligences to advance her learning, as many homeschooling families have done.

In addition to evaluating your child's strengths, you also have a variety of homeschooling approaches from which to choose, including the classical education approach, unit studies, Charlotte Mason Method, unschooling, and eclectic. Prospective homeschool parents frequently ask whether certain homeschooling styles are more appropriate for specific disabilities. The answer is no. There's simply no one standard that can meet the needs of only autistic or ADD children. To determine a homeschooling style, each family must evaluate the needs of the special child, other children in the family, the family budget, time constraints, and personal values.

Most newcomers to homeschooling follow a trial-and-error or sample-the-wares approach. All too often, parents are wowed into buying entire curriculum packages, only to have their child thumb her nose at it. Forcing a child to use materials because you like them and paid a small fortune only creates your own and your child's resentment. Learning cannot take place in an environment of discord. Take the time to get to know your child's learning styles, interests, and temperament before rushing out to secure all the materials needed to follow a particular approach. Learn about the positives and negatives of the various approaches by talking to other homeschoolers. Curriculum e-mail lists and bulletin boards are full of homeschooling parents who are usually very willing to answer questions and discuss learning theories.

Don't worry if the choices seem overwhelming and you just can't decide which one is best suited for your child. Your child will not suffer irreparable academic harm if you wing it for a while.

> Your child will not suffer irreparable academic harm if you wing it for a while.

Classical Education

Classical education is also referred to as the Trivium and the well-trained mind approach. Although the three philosophies vary, all possess similar underlying tenets. Classical instruction is accomplished through the spoken and written word, rather than the use of images, and all learning is interrelated. In classical education, the three stages of training a child's mind consist of, first, absorbing facts during the early years, followed by developing critical thinking skills through the middle grades, and culminating in learning to express one's self in the high school years.

A year ago, Carole, a Massachusetts mother, brought her learning disabled son home to learn. Their first curriculum selection proved a frustrating mismatch with her son's need for structure. She recalls, "We used the 'Five In A Row' curriculum where we would read a book and discuss one subject like geography on one day, followed by a different subject discussion on the next day. Michael's behavior and attitude became negative because he perceived this method as a lack of routine. He wanted to discuss language arts, social studies, geography, science, and math every day and in the same order."

Carole turned to her online support group, whose members suggested she read *The Well-Trained Mind: A Guide to Classical Education at Home* by Susan Wise Bauer and Jesse Wise. "What caught my interest was that it's a language-intensive, systematic, and academically rigorous approach to learning where all knowledge is interrelated. Finding the links among fields of study can be a mind-twisting task. A classical education meets this challenge by taking history as its organizing outline—beginning with the ancients and progressing forward to the moderns in history, science, literature, art, and music." Carole continues, "This approach gives us the daily routine Michael craved. He's calmer, more in control of his actions, and very willing to cooperate."

It's not just the structure of this approach that appeals to Carole: "We study one historical segment each year; ancients, Middle Ages, Renaissance, modern, and then repeat the cycle three times over the span of the educational years. During the early years, the child absorbs facts from the stories, and when he studies it again, he'll already be familiar with the topic and his greater maturity will allow for greater analysis and expression."

A classical education isn't the only style that emphasizes traditional academics. The Charlotte Mason Method also stresses high standards, although using a somewhat different approach.

Charlotte Mason Method

Charlotte Mason, a turn-of-the-century British educator, developed an approach based on the notion of establishing in children a lifelong passion for learning. The Charlotte Mason Method is a favorite with homeschoolers because it incorporates high academic standards, fine arts, and basic life skills, such as the development of desir-

CHARLOTTE MASON APPROACH

A Charlotte Mason (CM) approach suits the diverse learning styles of children, including higher-functioning autistic children. CM exposes children to living ideas through whole books (not textbooks), nature study, picture study, and other experiences. Rather than simply reading a poem about a daisy, they go outdoors, breathe the fresh air, draw the flower, and write down their observations and excerpts from poetry about the flower. Because autistic children tend to be concrete, the CM approach allows them to experience what they are learning.

Reading books is the heart of a CM curriculum. We read small chunks of a collection of books. Short readings can be very helpful for autistic children who often have short attention spans. Although autistic children are weak in auditory processing, they can be supported by tracking the fingers across the page, studying pictures about the subject, and watching videos whenever possible.

Most CM families favor math programs with short lessons that combine visual worksheets, real-life applications, and manipulatives. They gravitate to programs like Math-U-See and Making Math Meaningful.

able habits, using time well, helping others, and developing patience and respect. This approach uses short lessons to promote a child's concentration, and its developers also advocate the use of quality materials over those that have been "dumbed down."

Abigail in North Carolina, mother of five homeschooled children (three of which have special medical needs), states, "We use a timeline for history and science that we made ourselves and put into book form. This is similar to the Charlotte Mason Book of the Centuries concept of childmade historical timeline books. We also do nature journals that consist of documentation of our nature "rides," and including sketches as well as pictures taken, in-depth information on

Since our children are young, we do not test in traditional ways. Rather, we hold "exam weeks" periodically with essay questions, such as: "Tell me everything you know about . . ." Open-ended questions let the children give an informative narrative, rather than a disjointed regurgitation of facts. In the real world of life, parents want autistic children to engage in conversations, and these exams better resemble realistic expectations. When children are older, they can learn test-taking strategies to prepare for things like college entrance exams.

In my opinion, using a Charlotte Mason approach blends solid academics with learning in the real world. CM inspires children to create their own memories of their learning through homemade books (copybooks and art, history and nature notebooks). Nothing thrills me more than watching Pamela browse through her history notebook or hearing her announce that Beethoven is her choice for the next favorite composer to study.

—TAMMY, HOMESCHOOLS HER ELEVEN-YEAR-OLD AUTISTIC DAUGHTER AND EIGHT-YEAR-OLD NT SON IN ALASKA the rocks found, weather of the day, and cloud formations. My youngest son, who uses Augmentative Alternative Communications (AAC) to write, may "paint" on his device, and then we will print it out and paste it into his nature journal book."

She adds, "My older children are no longer using a Charlotte Mason approach, but I find they gravitate toward helping the younger ones learn along these lines. They also assist with the youngest one and his extreme medical needs and medical equipment so that he gets out for nature rides. I believe they like to reminisce about the nature walks of their younger days."

Moving away from the emphasis on seatwork that is often used in the classical model toward a more hands-on approach to learning, unit studies appeal to those interested in academics in a more practical, real-world sense.

Unit Studies

Unit studies integrate various academic subjects while concentrating on one specific topic. For example, the topic might be the ocean, and children would study it in science, read fiction about it, study the history of ocean travel, and the like. This approach allows children to thoroughly immerse themselves into one subject, something that schools simply don't have the luxury of doing.

My family's foray into homeschooling used unit studies. My son was six years old when he developed a keen interest in trains. We read fictional stories of trains, as well as historical accounts. We utilized small toy trains as manipulative objects to develop early math skills. A family friend who worked for the railroad took my son to work with him one day. They traveled from an urban hub to a coastal port with lessons provided along the way by another railroad worker (and former teacher) and my geographer husband. My son took photographs of trains, involved himself in craft projects related to trains, even listened to music about trains. We were able to cover language arts, math, social studies, arts, and music, all while studying trains. We pieced together everything from library books to videotapes in a very cost-effective way. While unit studies were initially beneficial in my son's early years, we eventually moved toward unschooling as he matured and started to play a more active role in his learning.

It is also possible to purchase prepackaged unit studies, as Rebecca, a homeschooling mother in Alabama, does. She uses KONOS unit studies and supplements math and grammar with outside resources.

"Because my three daughters are at different levels of learning, unit studies work great for us," she states. Rebecca is able to teach science, geography, health, history, social studies, and language arts all at the same time to her ten-year-old daughter and eight-year-old twin daughters, one of whom is learning disabled. "I don't need first-, second-, and fifth-grade science books, because my girls all study out of one book." But, she adds, "I do assign to my fifth grader a short report on what we're studying, while my second grader writes a couple of sentences and draws a picture and my first grader orally gives a brief summary of what she learned, followed by drawing a picture. We used this approach to learn the states and capitals. The cool thing was that my first grader, whom I was only hoping to familiarize with the states, exceeded my expectations by memorizing all fifty states and capitals, just through oral repetition."

> "Because my three daughters are at different levels of learning, unit studies work great for us."

Unschooling

If the thought of planning and acquiring all the resources needed for your child's education is making your head spin, consider the option of having your child choose what she wants to learn.

Unschooling is also referred to as child-led learning, interest-initiated learning, or natural learning. This "world as a classroom" approach was conceived and made popular by the late John Holt, a veteran educator and child advocate. So how do you get started as an unschooler?

If your child is young and has never been to a formal school, your days are most likely filled with questions and answers about the world around you, along with lots of hands-on activities, such as building things, cooking, and creating. To my family, unschooling has been an extension of those early years where we read aloud to one another, talked about everything under the sun, and participated in projects around the home and within the community. Although our son has matured physically and emotionally over the years, the underlying approach remains the same—he expresses an interest and pursues it either on his own or with our assistance.

On the other hand, if your child has been in school or you've followed a more structured approach to homeschooling, the first step in unschooling is to stay away from anything that feels like drudgery. Yes, do something fun! "But," you protest, "we're supposed to be doing something!" You will be. Go to the library, allow your child to choose books (without you pointing out what he likes). Read aloud to your child (regardless of her age). Visit museums and go for long walks on the beach (or in the mountains, the desert, or more urban environments). Act silly. Cook or bake something new together. Visit with someone who is unable to leave his or her home. Plant a garden. Unstructured time for your child to explore not only heals past school wounds, but it also allows the parent and child to realize that learning takes place anywhere, at anytime, and not only within a classroom. Doing what seems like "nothing" actually facilitates reclaiming your family life. Playing, creating, talking, and daydreaming all help to provide you with a valuable assessment of your child's interests and skills.

It's natural for many of us as parents to want to gravitate toward prepackaged curricula because we still maintain notions of what constitutes learning. We may also have the impression that these programs will make planning easier. Nancy in California started homeschooling by using curriculum and lesson plans with her five children, only to abandon the plans because they were "too much like what we were trying to get away from with school!"

"We've been using a curriculum, but it's only a small portion of what we do," states Susan in Louisiana. "Since my daughter learns much more during our less structured times, we've decided to unschool."

A North Carolina homeschooling parent, Carolyn, has been through the gamut of methods with her fourteen-year-old ADD and dyslexic daughter, who has always been home-schooled. "We used the Calvert curriculum for kindergarten and first grade, which was stressful for us. Next, we moved toward an eclectic approach, but changed to complete unschooling once I saw the benefits."

> Playing, creating, talking, and daydreaming all help to provide you with a valuable assessment of your child's interests and skills.

Kandie, a California homeschooler, has always unschooled her eight-year-old autistic son. "Unschooling doesn't mean without routines," she explains. "Autistic spectrum children need structure and not some predetermined test-taking and worksheet-writing program. The word 'structure' is frequently interpreted as school, but it's nothing more than a way to give the day some shape. Structure can be what you want it to be, whether it's getting up, dressing, eating breakfast, playing with sand, or climbing play structures. It's the child's personal structure or routine he has created. Jackson does best with a highly structured day, but one he's created that is also flexible. He reacts to his inner needs."

Some children know exactly what they want, and it's not textbooks or teacher-directed assignments. One veteran homeschooling father has not-so-fond recollections of those early years with his always-homeschooled son. "We really did try school-at-home. But, our son made it crystal-clear at five or six years old that he'd be doing his own thing." Robert in California states of his eighteen-year-old

Asperger's Syndrome son, "I have absolutely no idea where he's acquired most of his knowledge, but he's bright and imaginative. Well," Robert confesses, "except in math, but then I don't know many people who enjoyed math as kids."

Eclectic

Do you like everything you've read so far? Are you wondering how to incorporate all these methods into your homeschooling? Throw caution to the wind and try them all under the eclectic umbrella! Don't fret if your visual/spatial learner wants to try some of the classical approach. Anything and everything are fair game as an eclectic homeschooler!

"Our original approach was the 'canned curriculum' route," recalls Jill, a California homeschooler. "But we found it to be too restrictive and rigid. Needs also changed according to the children's developmental stages and styles. Dealing with various life circumstances through the years also necessitated a more relaxed approach." Jill's family now follows a blend of Charlotte Mason, unschooling, and some curriculum.

"We use an eclectic approach," says Erika. "For phonics and math we use workbooks, along with unit studies for science, history, and literature. My boys also like computer software, and they learn a lot from life!"

"Our homeschooling method is eclectic," states Tamara, whose son has ODD. "I cover some basics using books, although we never follow a textbook cover to cover. Most 'curriculum' resources adapt to individual needs. Mostly we read books my son chooses, and play games for language arts and math. But I wouldn't call this interest-initiated learning, because there is minimal structure. Reading, writing, and math have to be done daily, even if they're accomplished through games and reading library books." She recalls previous attempts using another homeschooling approach. "We started as totally unschooling, but it was a complete failure. My son isn't a self-motivated learner, and when given the freedom to choose, he chose to do nothing. Unschooling is not a good method for kids with ODD, because they try to argue their way out of everything. Rather than read one page, they would prefer to argue for three hours about why they shouldn't have to read it. I find that setting a minimal structure, with some flexibility, works much better for us."

Other Styles

Many of the practices used in school settings can also be applied to homeschooling. For example, both the Montessori and Waldorf methods have found niches within homeschooling. Italian physician Maria Montessori's initial school in 1899 was for mentally retarded children. However, once her successes became known, Montessori's methods were used in regular classrooms. Her basic philosophy was that each child possesses a unique life force, which guides physical, mental, and spiritual development. Montessori believed that children have an innate sense of independence, which guides them to examine their environments. Montessori methods utilize hands-on materials within the context of a consistent setting.

Waldorf education was the brainchild of the Austrian philosopher Rudolf Steiner, who founded the spiritual movement anthroposophy. After World War I, a local businessman asked Steiner to apply the aspects of anthroposophy to an educational setting for children. Steiner did so by emphasizing handcrafts and the arts, as well as more academic subjects, in an effort to develop spiritually aware and creative freethinkers.

Throughout the years, these two educational philosophies, Montessori and Waldorf, have been transformed to meet American classroom standards and, in many cases, have lost much of their original intent. However, many parents have revived and applied some of the basic principles to their homeschooling practices.

Ideas for learning activities are flashing through your mind, and your child is ecstatic about not returning to school. What more is there to do? You'll need to keep your confidence bolstered; it's time to tell family and friends that you plan to homeschool.

SIMPLE STARTING POINTS

✦ *Read books and articles on multiple intelligences and other learning styles.* Many of these books have inventories to assess your child's (or your own) intelligences. Embrace these theories to view your child from a new perspective. Cast aside those styles used only in classrooms, which portray your child as a failure.

✦ *Realize that your preference for a specific homeschooling approach may not match your child's needs or style of learning.*

✦ *Look at a variety of materials.* There are many outlets for finding learning materials. Request mail-order catalogs, browse through online catalogs, attend used curriculum fairs and larger homeschooling conferences. Many homeschooling support groups provide lending libraries as one of their services.

✦ *Don't rush into curriculum purchases.* This is a quick way to sour both you and your children on homeschooling. It's certainly tempting to pull out that credit card upon seeing all the wonderful materials available at a conference or homeschool supply store. Resist the temptation. Bring your child home, get to know his interests and strengths, and ask for his input.

RESOURCES

Books

Homeschooling Methods

Andreola, Karen. *A Charlotte Mason Companion: Personal Reflections on the Gentle Art of Learning.* Charlotte Mason Research and Supply Company, 1998.

Bauer, Susan Wise, and Jesse Wise. *The Well-Trained Mind: A Guide to Classical Education at Home.* W.W. Norton, 1999.

Brown, Teri J. *Christian Unschooling: Growing Your Children in the Freedom of Christ.* Champion Press, 2001.

Gardner, Penny. *Charlotte Mason Study Guide.* Penny Gardner, 1997.

Griffith, Mary. *The Unschooling Handbook: How to Use the World as Your Child's Classroom.* Prima Publishing, 1998.

Levinson, Catherine. *Charlotte Mason Education: A How-To Manual.* Champion Press, 1999.

Levinson, Catherine. *More Charlotte Mason Education: An Expanded How-To Manual.* Champion Press, 1999.

Multiple Intelligences

Armstrong, Thomas. *Awakening Your Child's Natural Genius: Enhancing Curiosity, Creativity, and Learning Ability.* Jeremy Tarcher, 1991.

Armstrong, Thomas. *In Their Own Way: Discovering and Encouraging Your Child's Multiple Intelligences.* Jeremy Tarcher, 1987.

Gardner, Howard. *Frames of Mind: The Theory of Multiple Intelligences.* Basic Books, 1983.

Gardner, Howard. *Intelligence Reframed: Multiple Intelligences for the 21st Century.* Basic Books, 2000.

Gardner, Howard. *Multiple Intelligences: The Theory in Practice.* Basic Books, 1993.

Schmidt, Laurel. *Seven Times Smarter: 50 Activities, Games, and Projects to Develop the Seven Intelligences of Your Child.* Three Rivers Press, 2001.

Catalogs

Homeschooling Methods

Charlotte Mason Research and Supply Company, P.O. Box 758, Union, ME 04862, www.charlotte-mason.com

Michael Olaf's Essential Montessori, P.O. Box 1162, Arcata, CA 95518, 707-826-1162 or 800-429-8877, www.michaelolaf.net

Steiner College Bookstore for Waldorf Materials, www.steinercollege
.org/bookstore.html

Multiple Intelligences

The Brain Store, 4202 Sorrento Valley Boulevard, Suite B, San
Diego, CA 92121, 800-325-4769, www.learningbrain.com

Free Spirit Publishing, 217 Fifth Avenue North, Suite 200, Minneapolis, MN 55401, 800-735-7323, www.freespirit.com

MindWare, 2720 Patton Road, Roseville, MN 55113, 800-274-
6123, www.mindwareonline.com

Zephyr Press, P.O. Box 66006-H, Tucson, AZ 85728-6006, 800-
232-2187, www.zephyrpress.com

Web Sites

Homeschooling Methods

Ambleside Online, free Charlotte Mason curriculum assistance:
317537.homestead.com/AmblesideOnline.html

Charlotte Mason Method: members.aol.com/BeeME1/Cmmethod
.html

The Eclectic Homeschool Organization Web Site (Christian Perspective): www.eho.org

Kaleidoscapes Unit Studies: www.kaleidoscapes.com/unitstudies
/unitstudyfaq.html

Montessori Foundation, 17808 October Court, Rockville, MD
20855, 301-840-9231: www.montessori.org/index.htm

Montessori Homeschooling: www.montessori.edu/homeschooling
.html

Unit Study Helps: www.unitstudyhelps.com

Waldorf Education: www.fortnet.org/rsws/waldorf/faq.html

Waldorf Resources: Information, Support, Inspiration: www.waldorf
resources.com

Waldorf Without Walls: www.waldorfwithoutwalls.com
The Well-Trained Mind: www.welltrainedmind.com

Multiple Intelligences and Learning Styles

Exploring Multiple Intelligences: New Dimensions of Learning: www.mult-intell.com
Harvard University's Project Zero: pz.harvard.edu
Thomas Armstrong's Web Site: www.thomasarmstrong.com

6

FAMILY AND
FRIENDS

© Photodisc

$\mathcal{P}$ICTURE THIS SCENE. You, your spouse, and your children have spent a pleasant but uneventful Labor Day holiday with your extended family. The kids have been playing games or splashing around in the pool with cousins; the adults have been chatting and preparing a meal. The family has gathered at the table, passed around platters of food, and settled in to eat, when Aunt Dumpling squarely looks your preteen son in the eyes and loudly asks, "You must be real excited about finally getting to middle school, aren't you dear?" Your impulsive son excitedly blurts out, "I don't have to go to school anymore! We're going to homeschool! Isn't it great?"

A quiet but perceptible and collective gasp ensues, followed by a long, uncomfortable lull in conversation. Dottie, your sister-in-law, a teacher's aide, breaks the silence, "I don't think that's such a good idea. I mean, you're not a teacher, and the schools have programs to deal with *those* kinds of children. How could you possibly help him at home?"

The floodgates burst open, and everyone offers opinions about the merits of public schooling, specifically for your weird kid. Predictably, all the noise has overstimulated your son, who's accidentally upended his plate into a cousin's lap, which precipitated a food fight between the two. Both children are covered with food and are screaming obscenities at each other. Part of you would like to express your appreciation to Aunt Dumpling and Dottie for initiating such lovely dinner conversation by smashing Grandma's Jell-o surprise into their faces. Mostly you just want to run away. Alone.

WHAT'S WRONG WITH THAT KID OF YOURS?

EVERYONE HAS AN opinion about how children should be raised, and they're not shy about expressing it. This unsolicited advice worsens when your child has difficulties learning or controlling emotions. Everyone's more than willing to tell you that your child needs greater discipline, is spoiled, and needs to buckle-down in school, and, of course, you're to blame for all of it. That you've decided to homeschool only compounds the accusations that you're a child coddler (as if that's a bad thing).

Flight or Fight

Our initial reactions when faced with opposition is either to flee the situation or to hold ground, battling to the finish. Neither action will improve an already difficult situation with your family, friends, and teachers. If you run from the arguments that detractors present against homeschooling, it tells them that you're still not completely comfortable with your decision. At the same time, if you either engage in a heated debate over your personal right to educate your child as you see fit or cite various public school crises, you're doing exactly what they are—trying to force another person to accept an opposing opinion. Remember, the debate started when someone attempted to foist his or her public-school-is-good views on you.

> Everyone has an opinion about how children should be raised, and they're not shy about expressing it.

The Naysayers

"Our close friends were concerned most with socialization. They felt my son wouldn't learn how to deal with the evils of other children's behavior, such as teasing and bullying," recalls Carole, who homeschools in Massachusetts. "My family firmly believes that we should move to a district with better public schools. What they don't understand, and I don't bother to share with them, is that such a public school system doesn't exist. I just verbalize how much we're enjoying our homeschooling adventures."

Robert, a California parent, states, "My parents haven't approved of homeschooling. They feel my son needs to be forced to conform; as my father likes to say 'it's a cold, cruel world out there, and the boy just needs to learn what it's all about.' While my wife's parents accept homeschooling, her extended family hasn't been as supportive. One aunt told my wife's grandmother that our Asperger's son is retarded, which greatly upset the elderly woman, my in-laws, and my wife. It has strained family relationships. My wife and I have essentially given up trying to explain our son's differences."

Beryl in Michigan recalls, "When we were in the process of moving, my daughter's teacher asked where to send the school records. I told her that nothing needed to be forwarded because we were going to try homeschooling. The teacher exclaimed, 'Oh, Beryl you can do better than that!' At first this was very intimidating. But now, I wish this teacher could see how far we've come. She was a wonderful woman who was defending her belief in public education. But she just didn't realize what a parent can do for a child with love and understanding."

CHILDHOOD BULLIES

Schoolyard bullies are typically viewed as a necessary part of growing up. When a child complains to adults about being bullied by other children, he is frequently told to "toughen up" or that bullying is good, as it "builds character." The Center for the Study and Prevention of Violence (CSPV) at the University of Colorado states that such misbeliefs about bullying only serve to perpetuate the practice.

According to CSPV, bullying is characterized by three criteria: it involves aggressive behavior or intentional "harmdoing"; it is carried out repeatedly and over time; and it occurs when there is an imbalance of power between individuals. There are two types of victims: the passive/submissive victim and the provocative victim.

Passive/Submissive Victim Characteristics

✦   Physically weaker than their peers

✦   Afraid of being hurt; poor physical coordination

✦   Poor social skills; difficulty making friends

✦   Cautious, sensitive, and withdrawn

✦   Cry or become upset easily

✦   Anxious, insecure, and poor self-esteem

✦   Difficulty standing up for or defending themselves in peer groups

✦   Relate better to adults than to peers

"Teachers, psychology professionals, family and friends all felt homeschooling would be best for my son, yet felt I shouldn't place such a strain on myself and how the whole family unit would be effected," notes Sue, a North Carolina homeschooler. Her five-year-old autistic son had been enrolled in a public school early intervention program when she removed him at the age of three. "Because I

Provocative Victim Characteristics:

✦ Exhibit some or all of the characteristics of passive/submissive victims

✦ Hot tempered and attempt to fight back when victimized—usually not very effectively

✦ Hyperactive, restless, and difficulty in concentrating

✦ Immature and exhibit irritating habits

✦ Disliked by adults, including teachers

✦ Bully students weaker than themselves

Finally, the CSPV cites the possible effects of bullying on victims:

✦ Painful and humiliating experiences can cause young victims to be distressed and confused.

✦ Victims lose self-esteem and become anxious and insecure.

✦ Physical injury or threats of physical injury may affect concentration and learning.

✦ Victims may start to view themselves as failures.

✦ Victims may develop health problems such as stomach and headaches.

✦ Constant devaluation of themselves may lead to depression and suicide.

—This information was obtained from the Center for the Study and Prevention of Violence, Institute of Behavioral Science, University of Colorado at Boulder, 439 UCB, Boulder, CO 80309-0439, 303-492-8465, 303-443-3297 (fax), www.Colorado.edu/cspv/safeschools/bullyingresources.htm

started homeschooling when my son was so young, I've always done his whole curriculum myself. It's worked out quite well for him, and he's working at the second grade level (according to the public school curriculum). The positive changes in my son have changed everyone's mind about our homeschooling. Success is the best stress fighter!"

BENIGN ACCEPTANCE

ONE RESULT OF the media's attention on homeschoolers who won national academic events and other positive reports is that homeschooling has become accepted by mainstream society. Consequently, many families report they don't receive direct objections, but some still believe that others view their decision to homeschool cautiously.

Jill, a parent in California, remembers, "Some people felt I'd have my proverbial plate too full to homeschool. I think for the most part, there aren't many detractors anymore. My mother is no longer angry, but I know she thinks it'd be best for the children to be in public school."

> Many families report they don't receive direct objections, but some still believe that others view their decision to homeschool cautiously.

Arnold, who homeschools in California, explains the reactions to his family's decision to homeschool: "There were some friends who felt that, by removing our teenage son from the school system, we were adding to, rather than solving his problems. The unspecified nature of his problem made it difficult to properly assess a course of action. But we did realize that the classroom environment was causing him emotional turmoil and, for that reason alone, we felt the change was dictated." Arnold's son was homeschooled for one year before successfully passing the state's high school proficiency exam. Although the family is still searching for insight into their son's learning difficulties, he's studying computer graphics at a community college.

Donna, a North Carolina mother, has decided to start home-schooling her three children, two of whom have special needs. She says, "We're sensing some cautious reservations amongst the professionals currently serving our oldest daughter. Because we're thoroughly researching and taking a conservative line in terms of change, people aren't blatantly objecting."

SUCCESS BRINGS ACCEPTANCE

MANY HOMESCHOOLING FAMILIES find acceptance after others have witnessed a child's successes. Lesa, a New York mother, agrees. She says, "Given time, most resisters have seen the improvements and realize it's due to the time, security, and dedication our son receives from homeschooling."

Erika in California states, "Family members see how well-behaved and academically well-rounded our boys' education has been over the past four years. We're still asked about putting our middle son in public or private school, but we just say we intend to continue educating at home. I think the boys' progress speaks louder than words, especially the eldest who's autistic, who's already surpassed most people's original expectations."

Converting protesters into homeschooling advocates was an unexpected side effect of homeschooling for Tammy, a parent in Alaska. "While people weren't openly resistant, I didn't feel much enthusiasm for homeschooling. Once they saw how well Pamela was doing, people became converts! Results speak louder than words!"

The seriousness of the situation before families begin homeschooling frequently provides a wake-up call for some. "Because the change in our son has been so dramatic, everyone has admitted that homeschooling was the best thing we could've done for him," affirms Rhonda, a Michigan mother, about her once-suicidal son. "He's gained so much in emotional health and a new-found confidence socializing with both adults and kids. Further, his reading ability has soared, and now, for the first time in his life, he loves learning!"

THE SUPPORTERS

NOT ALL EXTENDED families roil in disgust when you mention homeschooling your children. As my son approached kindergarten age, I frantically searched for a school to meet his needs. One day, my mother gave me a newspaper article about homeschooling and suggested this approach could be better than school. She's never wavered in her support of homeschooling. I suspect she also recalled my school years and the many times she had to challenge school officials to deal with situations.

Linda in Southern California was pleasantly surprised when her mother embraced homeschooling. "I expected her to criticize my decision to homeschool," she says. "Instead, she startled me by mailing materials she hoped would be educationally enjoyable to the boys. I have been absolutely astonished at the degree of support we've experienced from relatives and medical personnel."

In many cases, homeschooling is never an issue with extended family, as Nancy in South Carolina realized. "My parents understand the issues with Asperger's, they've seen my son's improvement, and they feel that his needs are better met through homeschooling, rather than sending him to a public or private school."

Tracy in California didn't experience any resistance from family and friends. "By the time I realized one of my daughters was dyslexic, we were well into homeschooling. If anything, I received support because I could give her more attention than she would receive in the school system," she says. Tracy has always homeschooled her two daughters.

A new homeschooler, Donna, decided her family needed to make some major life changes to accommodate homeschooling her son and two special needs daughters. They moved closer to her extended family. "My parents are very supportive about the idea and want to help. North Carolina is where we'll have ample family support, and it's a good state to homeschool." She adds, "Our three children are excited about homeschooling and living near grandparents, aunts, uncles, and cousins."

DEALING WITH POTENTIALLY DIFFICULT SITUATIONS

SO WHAT DO you do if you're not one of the fortunate ones whose friends and extended family share your enthusiasm for homeschooling? There isn't a tried-and-true method for convincing everyone that your decision to homeschool your children is right. However, many families have discovered ways to deal with detractors. How do you deal with the naysayers? Be prepared. Although you certainly cannot predict every difficult encounter, you can follow these steps to help reduce the discord.

Know Your Stuff

One helpful method is to thoroughly educate yourself about homeschooling, as well your child's specific needs.

"Initially the therapists at the rehabilitation center were skeptical that my daughter could get the kind of program she needs at home. They're supportive now that they've seen her progress. I think it's important," says Lisa of Michigan, "to educate yourself about your child's difficulties and develop learning goals. I have an educational plan for my daughter and because I keep track of her progress, I can give intelligent answers about her problems and development."

Sue in Arizona also recommends this approach. "My husband and I dealt with this issue by researching and learning the history of education as it pertains to schools, and by being aware of what's going on in the current system. We were ready for any questions family and friends might have on the subject and were able to address their concerns from a knowledgeable base. The key to discussing homeschooling with one who doesn't agree with it is to develop confidence about the path chosen. We read numerous books on homeschooling and education. My husband's degree is in education, so we also had the support of his professors."

Involve Others

Homeschoolers have discovered unique ways to get the point across to family. "Every six weeks, our children publish a family home-school newsletter that tells about their learning adventures," says Cherlynn of her three learning disabled children. "The grandparents feel our children are learning well at home. More importantly, they say our children are considerate, obedient, and a pleasure to be around. While their public school grandchildren have gotten louder, disrespectful, and more obnoxious with each passing year."

Stay Away

Large family get-togethers can quickly turn into a battle zone, especially if such gatherings overstimulate your child. One option that many families use is to simply stay away from these events altogether, or have one parent attend while the other remains home with the children. If that's not an option, consider making the holiday or other special occasion visit brief. Plan your arrival and departure at a time when there's a lull in activity. The short visit places more emphasis on socializing with others, rather than on your child's refusal to eat certain foods or his other perceived faults.

If you absolutely must attend the entire event, maintain a healthy distance between your children and the most vocal protesters. Don't allow yourself to be drawn into discussions about education, and if the topic should arise, gently direct the conversation to a new subject.

Prepare Your Child For "Those" Questions

Invariably, at least one person will be present who will try to use your child to "prove" that homeschooling isn't in the child's best interest. These rescuers follow a couple of basic approaches to undermine your homeschooling. The concerned individual will pay attention to your child, heaping her with praise and possibly gifts. Once they've assumed the "confidante" role, they'll show great sympathy for your child by asking her if she misses her friends from school or pointing out how much happier she could be away from her pesky younger siblings.

Although just as damaging to your parental role, the other approach is potentially more harmful to the child. The "pop quiz" is a favorite way to illustrate that you can't teach. If your child has already experienced school failure, his self-esteem is going to plummet further once Uncle Dick starts a rapid-fire volley on the multiplication tables. Many homeschooled children express a desire to attend school only because they don't want to be viewed as "dumb." Although most people realize schoolchildren can't answer every question either, the naysayers just cannot resist an opportunity to cast doubt on your homeschooling.

Help Your Child Develop Responses

Those wanting to rescue your children from homeschooling will generally take their arguments directly to your children. It's helpful to inform children that not everyone agrees with homeschooling. Take time with your children to brainstorm possible responses so that they can defend themselves from overly concerned adults. Make a list of statements and practice having your child respond to them.

Here are two statements to start:

+ "We haven't covered that yet because we have been so wrapped up in our paleontology studies."

✦ "I don't know, but I'd love for you to tell me what you know about the subject!"

My son prefers the smart-aleck approach and typically answers "those" questions with, "Didn't you learn that years ago in school? Maybe you need to brush up on that subject."

> It's helpful to inform children that not everyone agrees with homeschooling.

Demonstrate Through Convincing Experiences or Reading Materials

Invite a reluctant family member or friend to a support group park day or homeschool conference. This will allow them to see for themselves that homeschooling isn't just for weirdos. Lend them some of the many books that provide biographical accounts of homeschoolers' successes. Similarly, articles touting the benefits of homeschooling have become more common in popular magazines and newspapers.

Take It Slow and Easy

Don't try to wow the naysayers quickly. It has taken years for them to develop their current opinions of formal schooling, and it's going to take them a while to warm up to the notion of homeschooling as a viable educational alternative.

Maintain Your Confidence

Finally and most importantly, don't take the negatives personally. You've made the decision to homeschool your children because you are acutely attuned to their needs and interests. Rally the confidence that got you to this point, and hold your head high, knowing you are the expert in this situation. Don't let that confidence falter; you're going to need to tap into it on the difficult days.

SIMPLE STARTING POINTS

✦ *Keep reading about homeschooling and your child's needs.* Remember, you're the expert on your child, and experts stay abreast of changes. Knowledge helps build confidence.

✦ *Practice your "We're Going to Homeschool" speech.* It's helpful to pick three or four points from your list of reasons for homeschooling to focus on. Don't present long lists of reasons; it looks as if you're trying to convince yourself that you've made the right decision. Practice first in front of a mirror and graduate up to supportive friends and family.

✦ *Read books and articles on dealing with difficult people and dysfunctional families.* You'll learn additional suggestions for coping with those who disagree with your homeschooling. Learning more about family systems will provide you with insight on how families function successfully (or don't). Once you're able to comprehend the individual behaviors of family members, it'll be easier not to take their criticisms personally.

✦ *Encourage your children to write notes and send photos of projects to family members.* This will help the reluctant ones to see that your child actually does more than sit around watching television all day.

RESOURCES

Books

Dealing with Families and Difficult People

Bramson, Robert M. *Coping with Difficult People.* Dell, 1988.
Ellis, Albert, and Arthur Lange. *How to Keep People from Pushing Your Buttons.* Citadel Press, 1995.

Learner, Harriet Goldman. *The Dance of Connection: How to Talk to Someone When You're Mad, Hurt, Scared, Frustrated, Insulted, Betrayed or Desperate.* HarperCollins, 2001.

Satir, Virginia. *The New Peoplemaking.* Science and Behavior Books, 1988.

Homeschooling

Cohen, Cafi. *And What About College? How Homeschooling Leads to Admissions to the Best Colleges and Universities,* 2nd ed. Holt Associates, 1997.

Cuthbert, Cathy (ed.). *When Your Grandchildren Homeschool: A Guide for Interested Relatives.* California Homeschool Network, 1999.

Dobson, Linda. *Homeschooler's Success Stories: 15 Adults and 12 Young People Share the Impact That Homeschooling Has Made on Their Lives.* Prima Publishing, 2000.

7

ADDRESSING FAMILY
AND INDIVIDUAL NEEDS

In This Chapter

✦ Difficult days and nagging notions

✦ Seeking socialization

✦ Same parental challenges, different educational setting

✦ Benefits outweigh the negatives

✦ Just one of those days

✦ Connecting with your other children

✦ Maintaining the couple relationship

✦ Nurturing yourself

© Incredible Kids

$\mathcal{L}$IFE FOR SPECIAL needs families is typically a fragmented blur, with days running together and no clear end in sight. Most families shuttle among school, meetings with educators after school, and homework for all children. Then they have to get to doctor and therapist appointments and prepare meals. And don't forget that parents should spend time together as a couple and also nurture themselves individually. Because it's impossible to cram all these responsibilities into one day, most of us usually skimp on or ignore the last three items. Fast food is easy to grab on the way home from therapy, and it keeps the kids quiet. A spouse might get some face time in the morning or afternoon while the two of you arrange who takes which kid where. The closest parents get to nurturing themselves is sneaking a candy bar into the bathroom, locking the door, and eating it alone while the children pound on the door.

How would you like to eliminate some of these activities while also creating more cohesive family time? By homeschooling your children, you can eliminate the morning school rush, the meetings after school, and the homework. You can schedule medical and therapy appointments during daytime hours when your children aren't fatigued and cranky from a day at school. You might actually find time to spend with your spouse, and even by yourself.

> Homeschooling isn't a cure-all, but it does provide an enormous amount of flexibility within your family life.

Homeschooling isn't a cure-all, but it does provide an enormous amount of flexibility within your family life. This freedom allows families to plan most of what they do without school "consent." Ann, a homeschooler in Pennsylvania, recalls, "We had so much more stress when the children were in school. The school could hardly educate the 'normal' children, let alone my children, who were hopeless challenges for them. Programs for the child who is mentally gifted but learning disabled or mentally ill weren't available in our school district."

DIFFICULT DAYS AND NAGGING NOTIONS

HOMESCHOOLING PROVIDES COUNTLESS opportunities for families, but it can also create new problems, at least initially while growing accustomed to change. Are there negative aspects to homeschooling a differently abled child? As with most life efforts, difficulties homeschooling can be present, but so too are the rewards. Some homeschoolers may experience one or more of the following challenges. Others will not endure any—and still others will blaze new trails into previously uncharted quicksand.

Curriculum Planning Woes

Jill, a parent in California, says, "Sometimes the weight of having to plan curriculum for, teach, and enforce the education of five special needs children seems to be overwhelming. There are days when I lack both emotional and physical energy. On those days, I feel like we're not doing anything, then I feel guilty!"

Money Matters

Some families also experience financial hardships. "I've given up my income in order to homeschool. Because of this, I don't get a child-care credit on my income taxes for staying home," says Lisa, a Michigan mother who homeschools her fifteen-year-old autistic daughter. "I also lost my Social Security family support subsidy since autistic children must be enrolled in a state approved school program."

Absentee Parent

Homeschooling families in which one parent is frequently absent places most responsibility on the at-home parent. "Since my husband travels a lot for his job, I don't get many breaks from my kids," says Tammy in Alaska. "However, I find them more enjoyable 24/7 than the occasional meetings with bureaucrats bent on tying up my children's education with red tape."

SEEKING SOCIALIZATION

UNLIKE PUBLIC SCHOOLS, homeschool support groups aren't in every neighborhood. If parents and children have grown accustomed to large groups of children in school, they may find the transition hard. "Unfortunately, the largest homeschooling group in our area is too far away, and the closer ones don't offer as many activities," says Lee, who homeschools in Massachusetts. "My son's made one home-schooling friend, and it hasn't worked too well (the boy has his own special needs that cause him to have problems with other kids). My son has a couple of close friends who attend school, but it would be nice for him to have a homeschooled friend nearby."

Many homeschooling parents realize that socialization for chil-dren with special needs can be a double-edged sword. "My son is very immature at times and can carry on like a three-year-old," says Kerri, a South Dakota mother. "I've thought that being around peers might help him act in a more appropriate manner. But then, other children could mock him, creating frustration and withdrawal."

New homeschooler Donna, in North Carolina, speculates that her thirteen-year-old daughter will use homeschooling to further avoid social situations. "Because of her autism, she already avoids many social contacts. I hope the decreased peer pressure will have a positive effect on her desire to interact with others." It's Donna's hope that her daughter will emerge from her socially isolated shell once she's removed from the overwhelming school environment. Moving the family closer to extended family members who know and love the child may help her develop positive social interactions at her own pace.

The mother of an Asperger's Syndrome child expresses addi-tional concerns regarding her daughter's socialization. "She's been complaining lately that she'd like to go back to school to make more friends," says Linda of Northern California. "We've moved to a small mountain town where all the children seem to be in the local elementary school. I'm sure school wouldn't be a good environment for my daughter. All it would take is some upsets at school for her to start her AS behavior fits, then she'd develop a bad reputation among the other children at school."

Because no other local families homeschool, Linda has found other solutions to meet her daughter's socialization needs. "I've enrolled her in the 4-H program, and she visits with friends across town about once a week. She and her ten-year-old brother also ride their bikes into town occasionally where they'll often find other children. It's a very small mountain town and much less overstimulating than when we lived in the Bay Area."

SAME PARENTAL CHALLENGES, DIFFERENT EDUCATIONAL SETTING

MANY PARENTS POINT out that they'd face the same challenges regardless of whether their child is enrolled in school or is homeschooled. These parenting issues aren't specific to homeschoolers. "I'm stressed out," states Tamara in California. "But I've come to believe that I would have experienced the same level of parental stress even with a so-called normal compliant child. Having my sons in school would have had its own stresses. Homeschooling has its own stresses, even with 'perfect' kids. In fact, I sometimes have more stress with my younger son, who has his own different needs, but don't fall into the special-needs category."

Meeting the varied needs of a large family is also not easy, homeschooling or not. "Can a parent ever meet all of a child's needs even if you only have a small family?" asks Deborah, a homeschooler in Pennsylvania and the mother of nine homeschooled children. "I spend time with each child, but I might spend a bit more time with my Down's syndrome son in his schooling. I know I'll never meet all their needs."

Learning about your child's differences takes time. Parents gather information through books, articles, the Internet, and professional consultations, all of which are time-consuming efforts. Staying abreast of new developments, clinical trials, and seeking support are ongoing processes for most parents. "We've spent a lot of time researching ADHD and giftedness. But that's not been a bad thing, it's something we'd have to do anyway to understand the issues before us," says Nancy in South Carolina.

Frequently, we have trouble letting go of old feelings from our own childhoods. We see ourselves in our children, and we want to smooth their passage down the potholed path. "The only negative feelings I have are the ones I project onto my son," states Robert in California. "His Asperger's prevents him from having what I view as 'normal' friendships. At park days, I'll see my son alone, and I feel sorry for him that he's not involved with other kids. Later, when I ask him why he wasn't with the others, he didn't see a problem. He does care about others, but he's content with himself and his thoughts."

> We see ourselves in our children, and we want to smooth their passage down the potholed path.

Robert recalls his own childhood: "I never felt comfortable unless I was around other kids, and it's hard for me to understand my son doesn't feel the same. Homeschooling has provided him with feelings of comfort and security."

BENEFITS OUTWEIGH THE NEGATIVES

HOMESCHOOLING SPECIAL NEEDS children does present challenges, yet most families feel the benefits outweigh the hardships. "It can be draining. At times I think, 'wow, that big yellow bus sure does look good today!' The feeling passes quickly when I remind myself of the benefits," says Beryl, the Michigan mother of two daughters, one of whom has high-functioning autism with language disorders. "I am able to work one-on-one with my daughter at her pace and watch the development of her positive self-image and the exposure to the many activities and field trips."

Lynn in Georgia says of her learning disabled son, who is fifteen, "While I know my son's needs and learning styles better than anyone else, I sometimes think he'd benefit from a slightly different approach. I also think someone else might better reach him than I do." But, she admits, "Seeing the results of standardized tests made me realize that we are holding our own."

"I do my best to meet the needs of all my kids," says Kerri, a South Dakota mother of a ten-year-old Asperger's son. "With our other five children, their interests and skills are apparent, and they are quick to ask us to play ball, play a game together, or even read them a book."

Ann, a Pennsylvania mother whose son has ADHD, remembers life after removing her teenage son from school. "At first he was so relieved to be home and safe from being mugged. He needed to experience sleeping in for a while. When he realized he was actually going to have to do schoolwork, we had an uphill battle."

Ann's ADHD son did receive a state homeschoolers high school diploma and is now doing well, despite facing another bump in the road. "This rather laid-back young man, following graduation, was faced with the need to find work or be homeless and hungry. He suddenly discovered he had a fine mind and a skilled pair of hands," she recalls. "He's now attending community college in upstate New York, earning a double associate degree in both engineering and computer science, with plans to transfer in another year to complete a four-year degree in electrical engineering and software design. He's also working nearly full-time at Home Depot and has been diligently buying stock through the employee discount program. Who would have thought it?"

JUST ONE OF THOSE DAYS

EVERYONE HAS THOSE days when nothing goes as planned and anything awful that can happen, does. The notion of spending all day educating differently abled children at home can seem daunting. To many, sending the children to school seems preferable, if for no other reason than to provide a break for the primary caregiving parent.

Yes, some days are overwhelming, but we find ways to get through them. Sue in Arizona recalls her coping strategy from her bad days of homeschooling past. "My greatest relief came from having a wonderful and experienced homeschooling friend act as a mentor! Whenever I'd panic over my daughter not learning enough or we'd had an especially difficult day, my friend and mentor could help me restore my confidence, because she'd already experienced those feelings. I'd encourage other homeschoolers to find a mentor." Sue's epileptic daughter is now eighteen years old and thriving in college.

Some families develop alternate plans to help prevent difficult days. Notes Cherlynn, "On those days when you're screaming and ready to pull out your hair, you just have to close up 'school,' get out and just enjoy the day—tomorrow is another day!" As long as this isn't a daily occurrence," she adds, "you'll be fine. I have those days about three or four times a year."

At times, too, the parents of special needs children need to shift topics while they rethink their approach to teaching a given concept. Cherlynn explains, "No matter how much you try to get across a point, when the special needs child just doesn't get it, you can't push because it only creates more frustration and upset. It's better on those days to just back off and let your child recover while you try to find another way to approach the subject later. I've found unit studies work well since they fit each child's needs better than a regular curriculum."

CONNECTING WITH YOUR OTHER CHILDREN

SOME PARENTS ARE so focused trying to meet the needs of the differently abled child that other children in the family receive scant attention. These families must make a conscious effort to include all members in activities. "I make a point to spend one hour each day with each child!" says Jennifer in California of her five children.

Many parents find success by including their NT children in the care and teaching of the special needs child. "My eleven-year-old son is going to act as my teaching assistant as there'll be enough opportunities to build upon his skills," states Donna, a North Carolina parent, as she began homeschooling. "He'll enjoy and take pride in helping his sisters. I think any extra time needed for my daughters' special needs will be balanced by their many strengths." Donna's thirteen-year-old daughter has Asperger's Syndrome and her ten-year-old daughter possesses auditory processing disorders and mild mental retardation.

Planning special time for your children who don't have special needs is also helpful. "We've also set up mommy/son or daddy/son times for my younger son (who doesn't have special needs). He's learned chess, backgammon, and a number of card games. The two of us also do special science experiments. He has fun with this; sometimes we'll make things glow and my younger son will delightedly share the experience with his older brother." Linda adds, "Since my older son's difficulties have improved so much with homeschooling, I've been able to spend equal time with each boy."

> "I make a point to spend one hour each day with each child!"

California family therapist and homeschooling parent Michelle Barone notes that many of the sibling issues remain the same, regardless of whether a family is homeschooling or a child has special needs. The issues, however, are magnified when one child is not changing and developing at the same level as the others. She suggests a few points for dealing with your children who have typical abilities.

✦ Don't use the special needs child as the explanation for why siblings are not able to take part in some activities. Telling your NT son that the family can't go to an amusement park because his autistic sister will have a sensory overload there may cause him to resent his sister.

✦ Encourage your other children to express their feelings of frustration or anger as they experience them. Don't demand that they set aside negative feelings for the sake of the special needs child.

✦ All children should be able to nurture individual interests in their own ways. Don't force your NT children to regularly bring along their differently abled siblings. Tag-along situations are acceptable periodically when it's agreeable to all, but each child (disordered or not) needs to have time to develop individual friendships and activities.

MAINTAINING THE COUPLE RELATIONSHIP

THE LATE CARLFRED Broderick, a noted family therapist and sociologist, once said, "The most popular—and the roughest—contact sport in the country is not professional football; it is marriage." Toss in children, some with special needs, and tensions soar. Some parents blame themselves for somehow contributing to their child not being "normal." Others affix blame to one another for coddling the child too much or, conversely, not giving the child enough time or interest. They may make the same accusations about siblings without special needs. These concerns of parenting are not specific to homeschooling.

According to Michelle Barone, the parent who is not the primary caregiver is "only peripherally included in the child's life." The stay-at-home parent needs to learn to relinquish some roles and commitments by giving some tasks to the other parent. Involve the other parent without judging how he approaches a project or problem. In the case of homeschooling families, enlist the working parent to engage the child in an academic activity or hobby. Asking the child how she'd like to spend time with the working parent also helps foster a closer relationship between them and provides some regularly scheduled breathing room for the stay-at-home parent.

Couples also need to maintain their relationship. There are myriad marital advice books available, and some are listed at the end of this chapter. Psychologists and family therapists have cited a few key points for maintaining a healthy couplehood. Judith Wallerstein, Ph.D., author of *The Good Marriage: How and Why Love Lasts,* has outlined some contributing factors. Some are especially pertinent to those parenting special needs children: ". . . confronting and mastering the inevitable crises of life, and maintaining the strength of the marital bond in the face of adversity. The marriage should be a safe haven in which partners are able to express their differences, anger and conflict."

You're thinking to yourself, "Easier said than done." But you can maintain a working relationship with your partner by following a few simple steps.

- ✦ Remember your spouse is a different person from you. The two of you may share similar values and interests, but you're unique individuals.

- ✦ Respect your partner. This isn't to say that you must always agree with him or her, but show respect for your differences in opinion. Recognize and accept that some aspects of your partner's behavior may never change.

- ✦ Communicate openly without blame. Prefacing your statements with "I feel hurt when you . . ." expresses your feelings about your partner's actions and not his or her personality.

- ✦ Balance your need to unload your emotions with the unfairness of impulsively venting on an unsuspecting partner, which could overwhelm and shut down positive communication.

- ✦ Learn to listen. It's hard for one person to express emotions when it's clear that the other person is planning the retort rather than really paying attention.

- ✦ Be willing to forgive and to apologize.

- ✦ Remember to touch one another periodically throughout the day. A simple caress on the shoulder can brighten a harried day.

- ✦ Create time for the two of you regularly.

This last point is also referred to as "date your spouse." It's a notion that we all entertain, but rarely accomplish. Homeschooling parents of special needs children have a particularly hard time managing these dates. We're unable to plan these events for a variety of reasons, including limited finances if only one parent is employed outside the home, lack of child care, and plain old fatigue. If you find yourself in this position, consider alternatives to the weekly date. Grab snippets of time each day to spend with one another. Spend some quiet time in the early morning or late at night to talk about anything other than children and problems. Take that time to snuggle together in silence. Give each other quick shoulder or back rubs. This creates closeness and provides a bit of rejuvenation. Leave love notes for each other. My husband and I share candlelight meals on the patio while our son is safely indoors watching a video. While the food might be take-out, we enjoy a few quiet minutes over a meal.

> Spend some quiet time in the early morning or late at night to talk about anything other than children and problems.

NURTURING YOURSELF

THE LAST ONE in the family to have their needs met is the person who needs it the most, the primary homeschooling, caregiving parent. Parenting books and magazines are filled with suggestions to help you nurture yourself, but most of those tips won't work for parents of special needs children. The typical list will include hiring a babysitter so you can do something fun with your friends or swapping play dates with other stay-at-home parents. We often can't do these things because nobody wants to deal with our children's differences. Those of us who parent special needs children are in greater need of taking time for ourselves. Make a commitment to yourself to spend a few minutes each day for nurturing. It might not be a weekend getaway with your spouse or friends, but you can still draw renewed energy from ten minutes alone pulling weeds in the garden, taking a shower, or walking around the corner. If your child is very young or cannot be left alone, ask a sibling to keep an eye on her for a few minutes. Show your appreciation afterward with a special treat or time with you (without differently abled sibling) or, if the child desires, time alone for herself. Before you actually need such a person, search out a responsible neighborhood child or other patient individual to assist you periodically or for a short time on an as-needed basis. Don't wait until you're in crisis mode.

"I take periodic 'mental health days,' although, since my husband has taken on extra work, those days aren't as frequent as before," states Ann, who's been homeschooling for eight years. "A 'mental health day' is the time I spend reading, drinking coffee, and eating sugar cookies in Barnes & Noble or Borders. Depending on my level of stress and how much I miss my family, this can take from one to six hours."

Families may also find calm within the comfortable confines of home. "The smartest thing we ever did to alleviate stress was to implement a quiet hour in our house when the girls first started homeschooling," says Tiffany, a California homeschooler. "It was easy since we'd had naptime right before this stage of our lives. As the girls approached their teen years, all of us, especially my oldest daughter with the brain disorder, really appreciate having this hour to ourselves each day. My youngest gets a break from her sister, her sister has calm to recharge, and I get to rest up before the afternoon."

Erika in California finds comfort in communicating with other homeschoolers, many of whom she's never met. "Because I live in a rural area, it's far to find homeschooling support groups. Thanks to

TWENTY QUICK TIPS FOR NURTURING YOURSELF

- ✦ Take a ten- or fifteen-minute walk at a brisk pace.
- ✦ Spend a few minutes curled up with a pet.
- ✦ Listen to upbeat music using headphones—dance.
- ✦ Meditate.
- ✦ Pray.
- ✦ Jump rope.
- ✦ Keep a private "stash" of chocolates—eat one or two pieces.
- ✦ Invite a friend over for coffee or tea.
- ✦ Bake cookies.
- ✦ Do some yoga poses—take a lot of deep, cleansing breaths.
- ✦ Spend a few minutes working on a hobby.
- ✦ Watch a favorite video.
- ✦ Write a letter to an old friend you haven't seen in a while.
- ✦ Rearrange your furniture.
- ✦ Go out for ice cream—try a new flavor.
- ✦ Wear an unusual outfit.
- ✦ Read Calvin and Hobbes or another humorous book.
- ✦ Pull weeds in your garden.
- ✦ Read passages from a book that inspires you.
- ✦ Daydream!

two wonderful e-mail groups, I have some very strong bonds with people I've never even met in person! When things get stressful, I chat with my e-group friends and pray to God to lighten up the workload."

Michelle Barone agrees that a support system is crucial. "You must be able to 'unload' without being judged," she states, "whether it be with a friend, family member, or a therapist."

Finding other like-minded individuals with whom you can share joys and commiserate with over the rough spots can reduce stress tremendously. Online and in-person support groups are the next step in smoothing your path to homeschooling.

SIMPLE STARTING POINTS

✦ *Get enough sleep.* Everyone's inner clock is different. Some people need at least eight hours of sleep, while others thrive on much less. Figure out your individual needs, as well as your optimum times. Are you an early bird or a night owl? Resist the urge to force your body to adapt otherwise.

✦ *Look to humor.* Numerous studies have shown positive correlations between using humor and reducing stress or facilitating physical healing. Many of us use humor to cope with daily life.

✦ *Exercise.* Even if all you have time for is a daily fifteen-minute walk around the block or some quick jumping-rope in the backyard, regular exercise helps relieve stress and improves overall health.

✦ *Develop a close circle of confidantes.* Try to get a balance between homeschooling and nonhomeschooling friends. Each presents different perspectives.

RESOURCES

Books

Couples

Broderick, Carlfred. *Couples: How to Confront Problems and Maintain Loving Relationships.* Simon & Schuster, 1979. (This book is out of print, but is available at libraries and used bookstores.)

Chapman, Gary. *The Five Love Languages: How to Express Heartfelt Commitment to Your Mate.* Northfield Publications, 1992.

Stoop, David, and Jan Stoop. *When Couples Pray Together: Creating Intimacy and Spiritual Wholeness.* Servant Publications, 2000.

Wallerstein, Judith. *The Good Marriage: How and Why Love Lasts.* Warner Books, 1996.

Wellwood, John. *Journey of the Heart: The Path of Conscious Love.* Harper Perennial Library, 1996.

Wellwood, John. *Love and Awakening: Discovering the Sacred Path of Intimate Relationship.* HarperCollins, 1997.

Inspirational

Brice, Carleen. *Walk Tall: Affirmations for People of Color.* Beacon Press, 1997.

Canfield, Jack. *Chicken Soup for the Soul* series. Health Communications.

Chopra, Deepak. *Restful Sleep: The Complete Mind/Body Program for Overcoming Insomnia.* Harmony Books, 1994.

Domar, Alice. *Self-Nuture: Learning to Care for Yourself as Effectively as You Care for Everyone Else.* Penguin USA, 2001.

Harris, Rachel. *20-Minute Retreats: Revive Your Spirits in Just Minutes a Day with Simple Self-Led Exercises.* Owl Books, 2000.

Hoff, Benjamin. *The Tao of Pooh.* Penguin Books, 1983.

Kushner, Harold S. *When Bad Things Happen to Good People: 20th Anniversary Edition with New Preface by the Author.* Schocken Books, 2001.

Louden, Jennifer. *The Woman's Comfort Book: A Self-Nurturing Guide for Restoring Balance in Your Life.* Harper Collins, 1994.

Louden, Jennifer. *The Woman's Retreat Book: A Guide to Restoring, Rediscovering, and Reawakening Your True Self in a Moment, an Hour, a Day, or a Weekend.* HarperCollins, 1992.

Placzer, Melissa. *Chin Deep in Bubbles: Little Luxuries for Every Day.* Fair Winds Press, 2001.

Ruiz, Miguel. *The Four Agreements: A Practical Guide to Personal Freedom: A Toltec Wisdom Book.* Amber-Allen, 1997.

Ruiz, Miguel. *The Four Agreements Companion Book: Using the Four Agreements to Master the Dream of Your Life.* Amber-Allen, 2000.

Thorp, Gary. *Sweeping Changes: Discovering the Joy of Zen in Everyday Tasks.* Broadway Books, 2001.

Watterson, Bill. *Calvin & Hobbes* series. Andrews McNeel.

Web Sites

Homeschooling Humor

A to Z Home's Cool Homeschool Humor: www.gomilpitas.com /homeschooling/humor/105.htm

Homelearners Homeschool Humor: pub17.ezboard.com/fhome learnershomeschoolhumor

Homeschool Humor and Cartoons: www.geocities.com/uhomeschool /hshumor.html

Homeschool Teen Humor: www.eatbug.com/homeschool/Humor /humor.htm

Humorist Susan Kawa's Essays: www.mommarama.com/

VegSource Message Board: www.vegsource.com/homeschool/hshumor/

Inspiration for Parents of Special Needs Children

How God Chooses Special Parents, by Erma Bombeck: www.irsc .org/special_parents.htm

Parent Patch: www.parentpatch.com/SpecialNeeds/poems___special _needs.htm

Stay-at-Home Parents' Support

Mocha Moms: Stay-at-Home Mothers of Color: www.Mochamoms .org

Stay-At-Home Dads: www.slowlane.com

Welcome Home: Inspiration and Support for Stay At Home Moms: www.mommysavers.com/welcomehome.htm

8

HOMESCHOOL SUPPORT FOR YOU AND YOUR CHILD

In This Chapter

✦ The big "S" question: What about socialization?

✦ Different social needs for different kids

✦ Types of homeschooling support groups

✦ Support group challenges

✦ Do I really need to join a group?

✦ State and national organizations

✦ Can't find a group? Start your own!

✦ Other support group benefits

 $\mathcal{M}$ ost homeschoolers are reasonably comfortable that their children will succeed academically. After all, a 1999 study by the U.S. Department of Education indicated that homeschoolers scored, on average, eighty points higher on the SAT than did their peers who attended school. Beyond academics, however, is that sticky issue of socialization. To date there has not been any large-scale research that would allow homeschoolers the opportunity to tout how well their homeschooled children get along with others.

Because homeschooled children aren't in school, side by side with other children all day long, there tends to be a deeply ingrained apprehension that they won't learn to interact properly with others. Frequently, the concern is not so much the parents of homeschooled children, but others—grandparents, friends, and professionals—who, in turn, cause homeschoolers considerable anxiety. It is beyond my comprehension why any adult who cares about a child feels it necessary for him to be beaten by bullies, humiliated regularly, and forced to study concepts that don't make sense—all common occurrences with special needs children who attend public schools. For what it's worth, for those who worry that homeschooled children are "protected" and will not experience what many term the "real world," our children still encounter bullies. In addition, homeschooled children are not always delighted with every learning experience we "parent/teachers" present to them. Homeschooling is simply a different approach to learning that is not intended to avoid the realities of life.

THE BIG "S" QUESTION: WHAT ABOUT SOCIALIZATION?

WHAT, THEN, IS the big commotion about socialization? Many educators contend that children need to be around same-age peers for at least six hours a day, five days a week, 180 days a year to be properly socialized. Before 1852, when Massachusetts was the first state to implement a compulsory school attendance law, individuals were educated at home or in one-room schoolhouses. Although antisocial individuals undoubtedly existed, society wasn't burdened by packs of feral children scavenging through communities.

Current society has bought into the educational establishment's notion of what constitutes proper socialization for children. Why are educational professionals singling out only the relationships of children? Adults also pursue education, yet experts are not insisting that a forty-five-year-old must spend years of her academic life with other forty-five-year-olds in order to be "properly socialized." I know of no adult whose friendships are limited to only those of the same age. In looking at the entire lifespan of an individual, only a fraction of it is spent in childhood. If the first eighteen years are intended to prepare one for the next sixty or more years, isolating children in classrooms with same-age peers is certainly not the best rehearsal for the "real" adult world where interactions take place with people of all ages.

The same-age peer notion only serves to classify and sort children into classrooms based on the assumption that everyone born in the same year possesses the same skills and knowledge. Attempting to educate a group of children who are together only because of similar age is more of a classroom management tool and hardly an edict for developing socially acceptable behaviors or, for that matter, imparting knowledge.

Before 1852, when Massachusetts was the first state to implement a compulsory school attendance law, individuals were educated at home or in one-room schoolhouses.

Children may not possess the reasoning abilities of adults, but from a very early age, most are quite capable of choosing those with whom they wish to associate. Your eight-year-old child may prefer the company of her sixty-year-old grandfather during breakfast, while after lunch, she'd really prefer to pass the time playing computer games with the ten-year-old neighbor.

DIFFERENT SOCIAL NEEDS FOR DIFFERENT KIDS

MANY DIFFERENTLY ABLED children, particularly those whose disorders fall somewhere in the spectrum of attention and autistic problems, require completely different approaches to social interactions. These children generally possess delayed or inappropriate social skills. Placing an ADD or autistic-spectrum child with dozens of other children in a classroom and hundreds more on the playground further overwhelms a brain already struggling to make sense of social cues and mores. The child may misinterpret the words or actions of others and may misbehave out of frustration, opening himself up to disciplinary actions by school staff and humiliation by his peers.

Smaller group settings are actually beneficial in meeting the needs of these children. Interactions with other children and adults in semicontrolled environments (such as a small homeschooling support group) allow socially delayed children to play and communicate with others in a meaningful way. Modeling the behaviors of others with whom they have a connection provides valuable assistance in problem-solving strategies, learning to read social cues, and developing empathy.

Abundance of Social Opportunities

Shortly after removing their children from school, many parents are surprised at the variety of opportunities available for socializing. Parents often realize that their children have more time to interact with others in ways that are more meaningful than what a ten-minute recess provides.

A Texas parent, Elaine, did worry about playmate prospects for her eight-year-old high-functioning autistic son: "My main concern was trying to find opportunities for my son to meet/play with other kids (he's an only child, and I tend to be more of a homebody). As it turns out, he has many more opportunities now, since he's not exhausted from school and can socialize at his best time of day (he's an early bird). We've become much more relaxed and are closer as a family. And that's just made the 'school' part of our time that much easier."

Some families report that their children's lives are packed with activities and thus they have too much socialization. Many children are involved with scouting endeavors, and many homeschooler troops have emerged. Other homeschoolers are involved in sports or classes through local parks and recreation departments, many of which are developing daytime offerings specifically tailored to homeschoolers. In addition, many of these same children develop friendships within their support groups and want to visit friends between weekly park days.

Homeschooling support groups frequently serve as a hub for connecting families, thus providing avenues for socializing. These networks provide a variety of opportunities for both children and their parents. Some groups are large entities offering academic classes, sports teams, and other opportunities, which rival those provided by schools. Other support groups maintain smaller, more intimate communities.

> Homeschooling support groups frequently serve as a hub for connecting families, thus providing avenues for socializing.

TYPES OF HOMESCHOOLING SUPPORT GROUPS

TWO BASIC TYPES of homeschooling support groups are available for children and their parents: those providing face-to-face activities within a physical setting, such as a park and community or church centers, and those where the networking takes place via the Internet. Many homeschooling families use only one or the other option, while many others actively participate in both. Frequently, public and private school independent study programs (ISPs) will offer support groups, classes, and field trips to their members. However, it is usually homeschooling parents who develop and operate support groups.

Local Support Groups

Ask ten different homeschoolers to define "support group," and you'll most likely get ten different responses. In the most bare-bones version, there are park day groups and learning cooperatives. In addition, both categories may offer subgroups of structured and unstructured activities.

A popular tradition for homeschooling families is to meet regularly at an area park. Park days may take place once a week, once a month, or only occasionally throughout the year. Some groups have very structured rules and obligations for participation and may require families to commit to planning a certain number of activities or field trips within a prescribed time frame. Special needs families may not fit well in this type of structure because advanced planning is required, and parents of children with special needs generally don't know whether their children will be healthy or in a "mood" on a specific day in the distant future.

In many other park day groups, parents and children can simply drop in for play and conversation. Some groups rotate their days among a variety of area parks, while others remain in the same location.

Another popular style of homeschooling group is the learning cooperative (co-op). A co-op typically has more structure than the park day groups because the objective lies primarily with learning, rather than free-play time. Frequently, a group of parents will plan and alternate teaching one or more academic courses. Similar classes are now also being offered to homeschoolers by resource centers, some of which are operated by homeschoolers, although many are businesses run by others, such as teachers or tutoring services.

Not all activity-based groups model their structure after schools. Instead they may prefer to choose a general theme, provide materials, add a few kids, and let things happen as they may. "Setting up play days at your home or in a park where there is a focus that can bring them together helps. We had a science club for four kids at my house," recalls Lillian in California. "Each child brought an experiment (with all the supplies) and shared it with the others each week. The purpose was not to learn science, although they did learn a lot while researching and setting up experiments. The purpose was mostly to play. The science part provided a focus around which the rest of the play came together. The moms helped, but didn't try to turn the time into lessons. Activity groups can involve crafts or sports or any number of things, even fun math games!"

Online Support

Do you feel stuck because you want to connect with others but you can't find a local group to meet your needs? Or perhaps your child prefers not to participate in support groups? Remember that parents need socialization, too! If you have a computer with Internet access, you're in luck. Many homeschoolers feel just as connected when they're conversing with people online as they do with a local group. Message boards, chat rooms, instant messaging, and e-mail lists are extremely popular. There are countless e-mail lists for parents of special needs children; however, many may not advocate or even accept homeschooling. It's important to locate lists that cater specifically to home educators.

Online support provides information and encouragement to homeschoolers who might not otherwise have an in-person support network available. Through these support groups, those interested in learning about homeschooling in their particular state can easily locate pertinent laws and requirements. Many local support groups maintain e-mail lists or bulletin boards to keep up to date on changes in activities or to provide other useful information and resources. These lists also provide a sense of belonging to those members who may not be able to attend regularly.

Parents can access the online support and resources at anytime of day or night. This is especially helpful for those who find personal quiet time away from the children in the early morning or the middle of the night. You've had a rough day, your family is finally asleep, and

> Online support provides information and encouragement to homeschoolers who might not otherwise have an in-person support network available.

you want to connect with others, but at two o'clock in the morning? Yes, you can! Online you might find other night owls (or early birds in a different time zone) in a chat room. You can check a message board to read that other parents have had similarly difficult days. Or you can post a description of your day. Your instant message list notifies you when a friend is online and sending you a message. You can respond and spend half an hour chatting with her!

Those who have spent little time working with computers may initially feel daunted by the offerings of the online community. Take heart—computer expertise is not required, and all of the goodies are reasonably easy to learn with time. The homeschoolers who are already online are usually willing resources available to assist newcomers.

The online homeschooling support community does have its detractors, who cite as problems the overwhelming amounts of e-mail and periodic bickering among list members. The online disagreements (known as "flame wars" for their heated arguments) typically involve differences of opinion over hot button issues, many of which are not even related to homeschooling. E-mail lists have individuals (called moderators) who work to keep conversations flowing and the bickering to a minimum. Still, for this reason, many individuals decide to steer clear of homeschooling e-mail lists.

"I don't belong to any homeschool online lists, other than the one for my local support group. For me, 'online support' is an oxymoron. I don't feel supported by sifting through a zillion gigabytes of people's musings," laments Tamara in California.

Robert in California shares his distaste for online support groups: "E-mail lists make me crazy. I feel that some parents just want to dump their problems on a captive audience. Then, there are the ego-driven parents who live vicariously through their children by boasting about all of their successes. Sometimes I really wonder who has the special needs, the kids or the parents?"

Others aren't as critical as Tamara and Robert, but still choose to avoid e-mail lists. "I liked Aut-2b-Home while I was doing it," admits Linda in Northern California. "It was great to know there are other parents out there with the same kinds of problems, but I just couldn't keep up with all the e-mail." (See box on pages 142–143.)

SUPPORT GROUP CHALLENGES

ALTHOUGH SCORES OF homeschooling families swear by support groups, many others simply prefer to stay away from them. They cite various reasons for not participating in a support group, ranging from preference for smaller gatherings to poor health to parental desire to protect the child after hurtful experiences in previous groups.

Tolerated but Ignored

As much as we like to think of ourselves as open-minded and free of bias, the homeschooling population tends to mirror society-at-large. Whether the differences are physical or behavioral, many homeschooling families report their individually different children are not wholeheartedly embraced within support groups. In general, the snubs are covert, possibly because the families involved don't realize their actions. Individuals with physical or learning disabilities, as well as their loved ones, develop antennae highly sensitive to bias and are acutely aware of snubs. This isn't to say, however, that special treatment is expected. Parents of children with special needs hope that others will base their socialization decisions on an understanding of the children's true selves rather than their disabilities.

"We are tolerated, but pretty much ignored," states Tracy in Hawaii. "That's why our association with the local support group is loose. To be perfectly honest, only one girl in this group has ever been friendly to my daughter. Unfortunately, the girl and her family moved away."

Tracy is particularly frustrated by those parents who complain in great detail to her about how their children are desperate for friends, while ignoring her daughter as a potential playmate. Equally annoying to Tracy is her daughter being ignored by homeschooled children whom she's known for years in classes and other activities. As a result, Tracy and her children have opted out of support groups for the time being. "My daughter's already had more than her share of painful and unpleasant experiences," she cites. "I guess I just don't want to take any chances, at least for now."

If having your differently abled child ignored is at one end of the support group problem spectrum, being viewed with pity is at the other. Lisa in Michigan interprets her support group's views toward her and her autistic teen daughter as one of pity. In addition to pity, they've also faced the trauma of other children running away in fear. It's often difficult to tell whether children are truly fearful of how another individual looks and acts or if the "fear" is a particularly cruel prank.

Kids Can't Connect

Others find the challenges lay not so much within the support group, but within the child's different needs. Susan, the Louisiana parent of a seven-year-old gifted and dyslexic daughter, finds the socialization task doubly difficult. Although her daughter is highly social, she possesses interests not typical for a child her age. Thus same-age peers cannot relate to her or she to them. Susan says, "My daughter has some problems making friends, although she is highly sociable. She has many 'playmates' at our local homeschool group, but very few close friends. Her dual exceptionality makes her feel out of place just about everywhere." Fortunately, Susan's daughter has connected with another gifted child who doesn't view her dyslexia as a problem.

Still other children view themselves as outsiders, simply because they are new to an already existing support group. People involved in long-established relationships are frequently uncomfortable allowing others into their inner circle. Another equally difficult problem occurs when the newcomer is accepted into the group, while an existing playmate is pushed out. This latter scenario was one experienced by my son years ago. His best friend in our support group was enticed away by a boy new to the group who had "cooler" toys. My son tried hard to reach a compromise (no small feat for an Asperger child!), but the new child wanted the friend all to himself.

Coping with Support Group Difficulties

Dealing with the challenges presented in support groups can be a difficult task. We homeschoolers tend to be an independent and opinionated lot. Problems tend to arise within the group because we frequently view other homeschoolers as being similar to ourselves. We often feel that because we have all chosen to educate our children at home, we should all share the most basic preferences and philosophies. We don't. Within the homeschooling community, sometimes the only common thread is homeschooling. This isn't bad or good. It's just that homeschooling is a microcosm of the rest of society. You'll meet caring families with whom you have much in common, and you'll encounter others who are best left alone.

> Homeschooling is a microcosm of the rest of society. You'll meet caring families with whom you have much in common, and you'll encounter others who are best left alone.

The addition of one or more differently abled children (and their parents) into the support group equation can also increase the potential for a host of hurt and angry emotions.

Let's look at a typical homeschooling support group worst-case scenario. The other children in the group realize that your child is different, and they tease or bully him. This is very similar to what transpires on school playgrounds, only on a smaller scale. This situation could be viewed as an opportunity for some "controlled bullying;" after all, there's the common argument that homeschooling won't "toughen up" a child. You think to yourself that all of the children's parents are present, and surely none of the adults would allow anything to get out of control, would they? If you are new to the group, you may not want to create any problems by pointing out that other children are harming your child.

However, such occurrences have great potential to cause physical and emotional harm to your child. One individual tormenting another at any level is never acceptable. Your protests to the other parents may be met with swift resolution of the situation, followed by apologies for their children's poor behavior. Or, you could be faced by arguments suggesting that your son could benefit from a good tussle now and then. It can be heart-wrenching when the latter takes place. You may have taken your child out of school precisely so he wouldn't be bullied. Yet, here you are at your new homeschooling support group, your son is being hassled, and you're told not to worry or worse not to overreact! You may feel that of all people, these homeschoolers should understand and empathize with your situation.

How can you deal with these interpersonal difficulties while also protecting your child? Homeschool families use a variety of techniques to diffuse or prevent group problems.

Talk to Your Child

If you see behaviors taking place between your child and others that make you uncomfortable, call your child over for a private chat. Rather than asking her whether the others are bothering her, frame the question in a positive way by asking if she's having fun. Admittedly, your child may not answer honestly for fear of retribution from the others or because she fears you won't continue participating with the group. However, you will gain a sense of your child's emotional state and can act accordingly from there. Sometimes our differently abled children will actually start an interaction that quickly sours and they don't know how to stop it. When my son would experience these types of problems, we'd take time on the drive home, or even later in the day, to discuss what happened and how he and others contributed to the situation. We would then generate ideas as to how different actions could have resulted in favorable outcomes. It may take a while for new ideas to sink in with some children, but with practice, they eventually realize the benefits.

Ask Other Parents to Help

Very simply ask the parent of the other child to help devise a workable solution. Frequently, just telling others of your child's difficulties will help them understand. It's best not to sound accusatory toward the other child's actions. There are at least three types of parental responses to your request: (1) those whose children can do no wrong and your child is obviously the problem; (2) those who go through very limited aspects of solving the problem, hoping it (or you) will go away; and (3) those who are willing to work with you. Being able to address the problems between the children and to reach some level of compromise is the optimum outcome for all involved. Parents have the opportunity to model appropriate behavior to their children, who, in turn, develop the ability to generate alternatives to solve problems. If the parent is unwilling to recognize the problem, you may need to advise your child to stay away from those children who bother him or you may need to locate a new support group.

Cooling Off Time

Time-outs are a useful tool when tempers flare. "Sally was always (still is) one of those wild children at the playground," admits Sue in Arizona. "There were upsets, and I did find that so long as the kids were safe and not hitting one another, they sorted their differences out better when parents didn't become involved." Sue warns, "If they were hitting and not safe, however, then I would step in and just pull Sally away for a while for some food or drink, just to let them cool off."

It's so easy for children to be caught up in moments of play and forget to eat lunch or to take a break. This is especially true for differently abled children, who often become overstimulated quicker than the average child. One of our parental duties is to recognize what stimulus creates intolerable situations for our child.

Awareness

Many differently abled individuals find acceptance hard to come by. Often this is because long-held stereotypes are not easily overcome. "We've always worked hard to create autism awareness with children and parents in our homeschool group," states Tammy in Alaska, the parent of an autistic daughter. "Each year, we hold autism awareness training and a disabilities awareness workshop for homeschooling families." Tammy feels that the homeschoolers she's met have been receptive to her autism awareness talks, because parents want their children exposed to differences. She also feels that her daughter serves as an inspiration to other homeschoolers when they realize she has to work much harder than their own children to achieve the same goals. This realization can keep parental frustration in check.

Ice Breaking

In the perfect homeschooling group, veterans would buddy up with newcomers to help them find their space within the group. Unfortunately, this theory is not always put into practice. "We should all go out of our way to welcome people of all kinds, but I certainly understand that folks typically want to hang out with their current friends and acquaintances," offers Tracy in Hawaii. "Some groups have one or two people who are very outgoing and know how to get things started. I wish we could clone them."

Frequently, individuals within groups will try to foster communication by initiating activities. Unfortunately, our children don't always respond favorably to such techniques, either because they are shy or because their delayed social skills prevent them from appreciating the value of the interaction. Parents may wish to provide some awareness about their child's differences to those attempting to initiate such activities. Allow your child the freedom to proceed at his own pace. For example, your child may want to sit with you, or he may want you to walk around while he gets to know the new environment.

Support group members would be well-advised not to force activities or other children onto the differently abled child. We generally think that a nine-year-old girl would be happiest with other nine-year-old girls, and we try to pair children according to age and gender. However, an ADD or autistic spectrum child may prefer the company of much younger or older children who share similar interests. Again, follow the child's lead.

DO I REALLY NEED TO JOIN A GROUP?

THERE ARE NO rules that require you to join a homeschooling group or organization. Either due to personal choice or necessity, many survive handily without a homeschool support group. Some children have medical or emotional needs that require them to limit social interaction with large groups. Others simply prefer to socialize within the family or other small groups. Rest assured, your child will not develop into a social misfit if he's not in a homeschool support group. Provided you regularly connect with a circle of close, supportive friends and family, your child will experience interpersonal interactions with people of varied ages and backgrounds.

STATE AND NATIONAL ORGANIZATIONS

IN ADDITION TO the local groups and online support, there are also state and national homeschooling organizations. Although they may not be able to provide you with local support, they can be helpful for new, as well as veteran, homeschoolers. Organizations operate differently from local support groups; they tend to be charitable, not-for-profit organizations whose purpose is to educate the public and, in some cases, lobby government entities to preserve homeschooling rights. These organizations provide a variety of services to their members, including newsletters, legal and legislative updates, periodic regional events, and basic information about homeschooling. Many state and national organizations also offer e-mail lists and maintain Web sites with helpful articles and other resources, including referrals to local support groups.

> Either due to personal choice or necessity, many homeschooling families survive handily without a homeschool support group.

CAN'T FIND A GROUP? START YOUR OWN!

DESPITE THE GROWING numbers of homeschoolers, you still won't find a support group on every street corner. Most homeschooling parents either adapt to driving relatively lengthy distances from home to find support, or they start their own local support group.

Starting and running a homeschooling support group can be rewarding, overwhelming, and, at times, disappointing. To bring others together to share experiences benefits not only your family, but others as well. However, you're placing yourself in a position to anticipate and meet the expectations of others. This can be an onerous task, requiring an abundance of patience, organizational skills, and thick skin impermeable to barbs and bickering.

Find Help Early

Locate at least one other parent to assist with the group. Even if you think you can handle an unstructured park day once a month on your own, another individual's insight, energy, and willingness to receive and make phone calls, send e-mails, and just generally be there can make a tremendous difference toward a successful group. Make sure that you can agree to disagree with the other person, while remaining committed to the group. Also, determine whether this small group, which at the start may just be you and another family or two, will develop the goals and rules for your new group or if you prefer to wait for others to join first.

Look for Other Homeschoolers

To find members for your group, search out other like-minded families interested in a homeschooling support network. Ask the local librarian if you can place flyers in the children's section. Also, look for community bulletin boards in places frequented by families, where you can post notices with your phone number or e-mail address.

Plan an Event and Invite Others

Once you have found an appropriate number of people, organize your first get-together, making it clear whether this will be a planning meeting for adults only, or if you'll be kid-friendly from the start. The primary reason for an adults-only gathering is that the parents' attention can stay focused on the planning. Many groups, though, get the same result by conducting business through e-mail lists. If you're not using online communication, remember to print

ONLINE SUPPORT GROUPS OFFER REAL FRIENDSHIPS

Over the past five years, I've been involved with various online support groups, including "all inclusive" homeschool groups, Christian homeschool groups, homeschoolers of special needs children, and groups of autistic spectrum children (homeschooled and schooled).

The first group that felt like "home" was Aut-2b-Home. It started with a small group of about thirty families, which allowed us to really get to know each other and our families. The group has really grown during the past four years and now has more than four hundred members. On Aut-2b-Home, I found some really close friends that I could count on for emotional support regarding child rearing, marriage, and more. I could even ask some of them for financial help if I needed it.

I took over as list-owner of ASLearningAtHome (homeschooling Asperger's Syndrome children) in 1999. At that time, there were approximately sixty members, and we've since grown to more than two hundred fifty members. We've somehow managed to maintain a closeness that most groups lose as they grow. I consider the group to be a second family, and I am closer to some of the group

up and mail flyers to (or call) others with information about your event. If you sent your original invite more than two weeks prior to the gathering, consider the use of last-minute reminders.

Rules and Guidelines

Regardless of how informal you envision your support network to be, it is crucial that you develop some guidelines early in the group process. Determine how problems will be solved, especially when dealing with children who may have emotional or behavioral difficulties. The kids aren't the only ones who encounter interpersonal roadblocks, so be sure members than I am to my own family. We've discussed a variety of "dreams," ranging from having an annual moms retreat somewhere secluded to starting an independent study program for special needs homeschoolers.

The hardest part about an online support group is that it is only in text format. It's very hard to read emotions, and sometimes there are misunderstandings and hurt feelings. This usually comes about with different views on education, therapies, religion, or politics. A good rule of thumb in any online group is to not discuss religion or politics.

It's been said that online support groups cannot compare to the real thing, but I don't know if you could find many families in one geographic area that are homeschooling their autistic spectrum children, or any other differently abled child. I strongly suggest trying the online groups. Don't judge them all because of occasional bad experiences. If you find a group that's a wonderful support system, then stick with it through the good and bad times, because the friendships you'll find are worth it!

—ERIKA SCHRON IN CALIFORNIA, HOMESCHOOLING PARENT TO
THREE DIFFERENTLY ABLED SONS, AGES NINE, SIX, AND THREE

to establish conflict resolution procedures for the parents in the group. Don't forget simple rules, such as basic park day manners.

Have Fun!

Congratulations, you have created a support group! Take time getting to know the families in your new support group. Although you might not have much in common with some (except for homeschooling), you'll still find numerous possibilities for enjoyable experiences and, in some cases, the potential for you and your children to develop life-long friendships.

OTHER SUPPORT GROUP BENEFITS

AN ADDITIONAL BENEFIT of participating in support networks is sharing learning materials, curricula, and experiences. I have a "rolling library" in the trunk of my car—a box of books and materials that are available for lending to members of my local support group. We'll also have book swap meets throughout the year, where members will bring books and materials they'd like to sell or trade. New books are also brought to park days for our version of show-and-tell; we're not ready to loan them, but others are free to look through them while at the park.

> Kids aren't the only ones who encounter interpersonal roadblocks, so be sure to establish conflict resolution procedures for the parents in the group.

If you participate with an online support group rather than a local one, you can still benefit from others' insights and experiences with certain learning materials. Frequent questions that pop up on e-mail lists include: "Has anyone tried ACME-brand curriculum?" "We've gone through ACME-brand, Steps to XYZ, and we're still not satisfied—any ideas?" You'll find homeschoolers to be very resourceful, whether you connect with them online or in person.

SIMPLE STARTING POINTS

✦ *Contact a group member before participating.* Call or e-mail individuals from a few local groups to explain your family's situation before attending. Ask if other learning disabled or special needs children are involved with the group. Many groups seem to have one or more parents who "specialize" in this area—ask how to contact them directly.

✦ *Visit the groups.* If you're wary of how your child will be accepted, try to find someone to care for your child for a few hours while you visit the group by yourself to ask questions and get a feel for the individuals in the group.

✦ *Don't judge the group or its individuals by a single contact.* Upon hearing that you have a differently abled child, you might get a chilly reception by one person on the phone, only to attend park day and find a handful of truly wonderful, accepting families. Exchange phone numbers and e-mail addresses and stay in touch with them, even if you decide not to participate with the entire group.

✦ *Don't despair.* It takes time and perseverance to locate a suitable support group for your family. Stay in touch with support groups that may not have worked for you initially. Changes in your family or the group may take place, providing a different and workable setting. Look for an online group (for you or your children) or start one yourself!

RESOURCES

Books

Houk, Katherine. *Creating a Cooperative Learning Center: An Idea Book for Homeschooling Families.* Longview Publishing, 2000.

Koeser, Linda, and Lori Marse. *The Complete Guide to Successful Coping for Homeschooling Families.* Available through Greenleaf Press, 2761 Hwy 109 North, Lebanon, TN 37087, 800-311-1508, www.greenleafpress.com.

Homeschooling Special Needs E-Mail Lists

Alexconnecting: groups.yahoo.com/group/Alexconnecting

Asperger's Syndrome Learning At Home: groups.yahoo.com/group/ASLearningAtHome

Aut-2b-Home (autism): Send request to aut-2b-home-request@maelstrom.stjohns.edu

Home Educating Alternative Learners (HEAL): groups.yahoo.com
/group/CA-HEAL

Homeschooling ADHD & Gifted Children: groups.yahoo.com
/group/ADHDandgifted

Homeschooling Autistic Children: groups.yahoo.com/group/aut-home
-fam

Homeschooling Kids with Disabilities: groups.yahoo.com/group
/hkwd

Homeschooling Language Impaired Children: groups.yahoo.com
/group/HomeschoolLI

Homeschooling Tourette's Children: ourworld.cs.com/TouretteEmail
/index.htm

Newsletters

*At Our Own Pace Newsletter for Homeschooling Families with Special
Needs,* Jean Kulczyk, 102 Willow Drive, Waukengan, IL 60087,
www.vastnetwork.org/AOOP.html

The Link, 587 N. Ventu Park Road, Suite F-911, Newbury Park, CA
91320, 888-470-4513, www.homeschoolnewslink.com

Web Sites

About.com Homeschooling Support Groups and Organizations:
homeschooling.about.com/cs/supportgroups/

A to Z Home's Cool Regional and World Wide Homeschooling Support: www.gomilpitas.com/homeschooling/regional/Region.htm

Home Education Learning Magazine (HELM) Online Support Groups'
Listing: www.helmonline.com/pages/res/elists/elistsindex.shtml

Home Education Magazine (HEM) Support Group Area: www.home
-ed-magazine.com/wlcm_groups.html

National Home Education Network's (NHEN) Support Group:
www.nhen.org/nhen/pov/support/

Netiquette Rules: www.albion.com/netiquette/corerules.html

9

LEARNING MATERIALS

© Photodisc

𝒯HE LEARNING MATERIALS that you use in your homeschool can include a variety of resources, whether you prefer to practice school-at-home or follow a more eclectic approach. Unless you are enrolled in a state-operated homeschooling program, you have quite a bit of flexibility in deciding what materials work best for your children.

Choosing from among the many resources can be daunting, and you may be tempted to go on a buying spree. Don't do it: The new homeschooler doesn't need to break the bank getting started. Resist the pressure from advertisers touting the latest products *guaranteed* to teach your child to read. The programs are usually expensive, and you're made to feel as if you're a neglectful parent for not purchasing them on the spot. Remember, though, programs don't come with guarantees, and you need to use whatever works best for your child—starting with inexpensive and easily accessible resources.

THE SIMPLE THINGS

MOST OF A homeschooler's learning material needs can be addressed simply. A few basic tools can carry you through years of homeschooling. Your best resource for books, magazines, and videos is the local public library. Even if your child doesn't yet read, take her to the library, tell her to select some books (of her choosing—parental nudging is generally not necessary), check them out, and enjoy reading them together! Many libraries also have children's and nature videos available.

> Cooking and baking together are great ways to teach basic math skills to all ages of homeschooled children.

Regardless of your child's age, provide many arts and crafts supplies, such as crayons, colored pencils, waterproof markers, different kinds of paper, safety scissors, glue, tape, and rubber cement. Doing so allows your child to not only express his creativity, but also to develop fine motor skills.

Manipulatives are also an inexpensive and useful tool for math, logic, and fun. Many teacher supply stores and catalogs sell small plastic figures (bears, cars, trains, and such) in bulk. Children who have difficulty understanding the abstract notions behind math often find the concepts easier to grasp when they have concrete objects to work with. My son especially enjoyed working with the edible manipulatives, such as pieces of cereal, raisins, and peanuts. Get a set of measuring cups and spoons that are easy for your child to read. Cooking and baking together are great ways to teach basic math skills to all ages of homeschooled children.

More academic pursuits can be accomplished in a manner equally as simple, using a basic course of study outline (scope and sequence) and instructing your child in how to use reference materials.

Scope and Sequence

Parents new to homeschooling tend to fret that they won't know what subjects to cover at specific grade levels. Such requirements depend on your state laws. Check your state's department of education Web site for grade-level guidelines. In many states, there are no prescribed courses of study by grade level, unless your child is enrolled in a public independent study program (ISP). In California, for example, independent homeschoolers (those not enrolled with public programs) follow an expansive and vague outline detailed for private schools. Although it doesn't provide much guidance, it does offer a tremendous amount of freedom to pursue studies more related to interest than to a government-prescribed framework.

HOW WE DID IT

When my son was six years old, he had an unusual interest in animals, and he wanted to learn about all kinds. I taught him how to read by making lists of animals that start with each letter of the alphabet. "P" was his favorite. He could name thirty-six animals that started with this letter. His current fascination is with geography. He can name all the countries of Africa and South America and knows all the country capitals. He goes to bed at night reading his atlas. We studied Magellan and learned geography just by reading about where Magellan traveled. My son may not know a lot about a variety of subjects, but he is a deep thinker, he loves to learn, and he has become very knowledgeable about specific subjects. And, that's ok with us.

—KERRI, SOUTH DAKOTA, MOTHER TO A TEN-YEAR-OLD ASPERGER'S SYNDROME SON

Even if your state doesn't set forth grade-specific guidelines, some parents like to have an understanding of what subjects are taught at what time. Scope and sequence guidelines are available to provide this information. One of the most popular scope and sequence guidelines is compiled by the World Book Company for grades K–12. This slim pamphlet is available for a dollar or less through most curriculum retailers or for free on the World Book Web site (www.worldbook .com/ptrc/html/curr.htm). The pamphlet lists subjects and content that are typically taught at each grade level. Many of the general curriculum guides also provide scope and sequence lists, as do many curriculum companies and homeschooling Web sites.

The Core Knowledge series by E. D. Hirsch Jr., *What Your X-Grader Needs to Know,* provides a popular guideline for homeschoolers. The theory behind the Core Knowledge movement is that it provides a well-rounded education, creating a society of literate writers and speakers. It is believed that prosperous opportunities will be afforded to those who possess cultural literacy.

It's best to use a scope and sequence or the Core Knowledge books as reference materials and *not* as strict guidelines that must be followed at all costs. School-related tools, such as grade level standards, letter grades, and standardized tests, should be viewed within the context they were intended to be used—as classroom management tools. These items may or may not find their way into your homeschooling, depending on your educational philosophies. Keep in mind that children learning at home need not be constrained by the same practices found in traditional school settings.

Build a Home Library

Many homeschooling families (my own included) build a small to moderate library of reference books. Fewer than a dozen books, plus access to a good Internet search engine, will help you to field all of those "why?" questions that your child asks.

Books published by Usborne and Dorling Kindersley are favorites among homeschoolers because they're colorful, easy to read, and reasonably priced. After our initial failed attempt to implement school-at-home, we found everything we needed for math and reading in the primary years in two books from the Usborne Parents' Guide series: *Help Your Child Learn Number Skills* and *Help Your Child Learn to Read.* Each book retails for less than ten dollars. These two volumes, many story and picture books, manipulatives, and art supplies met my son's needs for years.

As my son has matured, our library has expanded. We've added question-and-answer type reference books, such as *The Handy Science Answer Book*, as well as titles of a more encyclopedic nature, such as *Dorling Kindersley's Ultimate Visual Dictionary of Science* and the *Merriam Webster Geographical Dictionary.* Other useful books have included James W. Loewen's *Lies My Teacher Told Me: Everything Your American History Textbook Got Wrong* and *Woe Is I: The Grammarphobe's Guide to Better English* by Patricia T. O'Conner.

If we can't find answers to our questions in any of our books, we look to an Internet search engine, such as Google.com, Dogpile.com, or the old standby Yahoo.com. In addition, Web sites like *How Stuff Works* are bookmarked for quick access.

The traditional definition of an educated child is one who can memorize and regurgitate facts when called upon. It's time to reframe that notion to the realization that learning is a life-long process, and the ability to seek desired information is a more useful skill than being able to bark out answers like a trained seal.

FAVORITE LEARNING RESOURCES AND SUPPLIERS

PREFERENCES FOR LEARNING materials are as varied as homeschooling styles. Most of us spent our childhoods memorizing useless data from staid textbooks, listening to teachers lecture, and occasionally, as a treat, getting to do hands-on activities. Unfortunately, our children's lifeless learning experiences mirror our own. Sometimes it seems that the prevalent notion maintains that learning must inflict pain, boredom, confusion, or all three combined. Why? Learning should be rewarding, expansive—and yes, fun!

> Most of us spent our childhoods memorizing useless data from staid textbooks, listening to teachers lecture, and occasionally, as a treat, getting to do hands-on activities.

Special needs homeschoolers have the freedom to break away from traditional learning tools. We use whatever works for our children's unique intelligences and challenges, whether it's a prepackaged curriculum or cartoon characters. "Calvin and Hobbes books," muses LJ of Oregon, "keep kids' attention, and kids read the books again and again." My own son is also an alumnus of the "Calvin and Hobbes Curriculum," and people seemed horrified that I would even consider utilizing something humorous and fun as a tool for his education. The same people were also eventually completely in awe of my son's vast vocabulary, which was gleaned from reading those books. The books also provided us with numerous opportunities to discuss proper and unacceptable behaviors in a way that my son understood.

Variety Is the Key

Many homeschoolers opt for a variety of learning materials rather than one prepackaged curriculum. Although one particular company may have a fantastic language arts approach, you or your child may not "click" with the math program. Therefore, families seem to find the most success by picking and choosing materials from various sources for different subjects.

"We've had success using *Wordsmith Apprentice, Learning Language Arts Through Literature (LLATL), Moving With Math,* and lots of manipulatives and computer time," states Rhonda in Michigan.

"Using *Building Thinking Skills* has been helpful because it builds on one of his existing talents." She adds, "He now writes short prose and poetry with the help of *Wordsmith Apprentice* and *LLATL,* along with big doses of encouragement and patience. It's a major miracle for him just to get words on paper."

A combination of careful planning, a patient tutor, and a selection of good books complete the curriculum for Kerri's ten-year-old son. "We use *Bob Jones Math,* because its colorful pages work better for him. We were also able to find a math tutor who could take the time to go over (and over) math facts with him until they were mastered. We also use *Learning Language Arts Through Literature* and *Spelling Power.* He does so much better when we have regular schedules, consistency, and, yes, workbooks. My son helps plan his own goals and the subjects and books he wants to study. If a particular curriculum or textbook is frustrating for him, we can put it aside and find something else. Sometimes the frustration isn't worth it!"

"My eighteen-year-old Asperger's Syndrome son doesn't like to write. It's been the one hard thing we have to overcome," admits Dawn in Wisconsin. "*Write Source* helped to inspire his thinking process and created the ability for him to understand how he needs to write to communicate his thoughts to others. The book is written in a fun, cartoony, colorful manner, and he has found it quite helpful in this challenge."

Cost Effective

Because many homeschoolers are single-income families, they need to keep the cost of learning materials to a minimum without sacrificing quality.

We purchase our books primarily by mail order through the Quality Paperback Book Club (QPBC). Many of our "finds" included softcover books that are only available through this club (retailers still had hard cover). After purchasing a certain dollar amount, we'd accrue points to order books for only the price of shipping. I'll frequently visit retail bookstores to look for interesting titles, and then order them through the book club. If I can't find a desired book in QPBC's collection, I'll buy through Booksense.com, the American's Booksellers Association's link to independent book outlets.

Many of the chain bookstores issue educator's discount cards for academically related materials. Some of them balk at providing homeschoolers with these perks and will ask for a teachers' union card or school pay stub for "proof" of your authenticity as a teacher. Fortunately, most just issue the card with no questions asked.

Another discount opportunity can be found on homeschooling catalog Web sites. Some of these sites offer "online only" sales to those who regularly check the Web sites or who subscribe to free, e-mail newsletters. Other homeschoolers use a mail order outlet where they receive good service and prices.

"I buy most of my homeschooling materials from Shekinah Curriculum Cellar because of their great prices and sales," says Erika in California. "They will also price match any other company if you tell them about it."

Tamara in California suggests another mail-order outlet. "Rainbow Resources catalog is the cheapest place to order from, if you know what you are looking for."

> Children (and their parents) love games and unique doo-dads, and there's no reason why these materials can't be used to learn.

Unconventional Learning Tools

Children (and their parents) love games and unique doo-dads, and there's no reason why these materials can't be used to learn. While games may seem too much like play, with very little academic value, they do provide a variety of skills, especially for the differently abled child. Learning to take turns with others benefits a child's social skills. Games also require the ability to understand instructions and develop playing strategies.

Similarly, hands-on activities speak to the needs of many children (and adults!) who learn best kinesthetically. A child who has difficulty understanding scientific or mathematical abstractions may experience more success once she's able to wrap her hands around a concrete example.

Don't forget that fun can also be educational!

"I love Timberdoodle with their oddball products!" exclaims Rhonda. "They just fit my son, and what kid wouldn't like to make a dynamo powered flashlight?"

Kathy in California finds television to be a useful tool in home-schooling her fourteen-year-old ADD son. "We like educational television programs, like CNN, the Discovery Channel, A&E, and the History Channel. You can register at their Web sites as an educator, and they'll send you all kinds of free resources and goodies to go along with their programs and lesson plans."

CHOOSING A PREPACKAGED CURRICULUM

MANY NEWCOMERS TO homeschooling look to the prepackaged curriculum as an easier way to make the transition from traditional schooling to home education. Numerous companies publish these curricula, and their offerings are varied. The most frequently cited reason for using a preplanned curriculum is that it provides a "safety net" for the parent by including everything needed to homeschool. You'll receive books (including teacher's guides), worksheets, and tests. Many curriculum companies also provide teacher services where your child's work is sent to a teacher, who reviews, grades, and offers comments to the homeschooling parent. Independent study programs are frequently connected with curriculum companies. These services typically consist of record keeping, report cards, a high school diploma, and transcripts.

Religious families can purchase suitable materials that adhere to the principles specific to their faiths, which are available from multiple companies.

LEARNING ALONGSIDE YOUR CHILDREN

We don't use a homeschool curriculum. Instead, we rely on a variety of resources. I might get a teaching module from Carolina Science, where they have great things like butterflies you can raise or archeological kits. Most museums have a store, and many of the more creative things we've enjoyed came from those stores. For example, the Jet Propulsion Laboratory (JPL) has a series of fantastic outer space pictures, which are available free to anyone who asks.

Hands-on experiences have been beneficial, especially for science. We're currently using kits that include DNA and microscope studies. We've built robots, and my oldest son built wooden marble mazes with his dad.

We've also worked on projects for Boy Scout badges. My younger son threw casts and sculpted with rock and clay for the sculpture badge. He also organized a beautiful planting area in the backyard for his Boy Scout Family badge. I like the double reward—working toward earning a badge plus the satisfaction of living with their accomplishments.

Expense is the primary disadvantage of using a prepackaged curriculum. The average full-service curriculum company can cost into the thousands of dollars. However, most will sell only the books, without the record-keeping or teacher services, which significantly lowers the price tag.

Computer Curriculum

Massachusetts homeschooler Carole says, "I've been very impressed with the Alpha Omega *Switched on Schoolhouse* computer curriculum. It allows only one question to be available at a time, so the child no longer experiences 'whole page anxiety.' No writing is re-

PBS television periodically has some awesome series. We watched one on the California missions, and we've been visiting several of them. Another series was on the history of California, which was more graphic than I wanted them to be exposed to at this point. I was able to take aspects of it and combine it with information located on the Internet. There's so much online, and each boy has his own computer with Internet access.

I'm working on a master's degree in research, and my sons help me review for tests. I recently took my younger son with me to a psychology class lecture when a visiting specialist spoke on how the eye works (specifically what it doesn't see). My son was able to ask numerous questions.

Primarily, I look for fun materials that will give the kids exposure to subjects while also preparing them for when they hit college. I have been learning a lot, right along with my sons!

—LINDA IN SOUTHERN CALIFORNIA

quired for this program, just typing. We can save the work on the computer, it's easy to grade, and no clutter is produced because we only print grades."

Standard Favorites

Dawn in Wisconsin found that a preplanned curriculum helped her son learn the basics that his previous school neglected to teach. "Using Alpha Omega, we were able to pinpoint areas in Josh's learning that were not covered when he was in public school. This curriculum enabled us to fill in the gaps without putting him through all seven years again. When he finally caught up to grade level," she continued, "we added other curricula, but we started with this one, and I think it made all the difference in the world to his education."

One of the oldest correspondence courses still receives high marks. "The Calvert School curriculum incorporates many special education ideas without labeling them as such," says LJ in Oregon.

PREPARING FOR COLLEGE AND BEYOND

ONE OF THE most common concerns of homeschooling parents is whether their children will be adequately prepared for college. The same concern is true for parents of differently abled children, but with the added worry that their children's disabilities could prevent them from a college education altogether. Preparation for differently abled students is the same as for others, but most colleges have special admissions procedures (similar to those for athletes). Your child's application will go through the disabled student services office, rather than through the main admissions office. You'll most likely need to visit the campus for testing (if your child doesn't already have a formal diagnosis) and for interview sessions.

Community colleges are a good starting point for all students, not just those with difficulties learning. The first two years of general education studies at a community college, as well as many introductory major classes, can be transferred to a university. For children with learning difficulties, it's often easier to be admitted to a four-year school as a junior rather than as a freshman. An added bonus is that the tuition at a two-year college is lower, which allows for freedom in class experimentation. I've found that most community college professors who teach introductory courses are more involved with their students than are the publish-or-perish university professors who tend to view basic overview classes as "dummy" courses.

If your differently abled child is interested in attending college, contact the disabled student services office of the desired campus for information about admission procedures and available services. These programs serve students with both physical and learning disabilities by providing accommodations, such as books on tape, untimed proctored tests, and other assistance to facilitate learning. There's also a small but growing body of books specifically geared toward the college-bound student with disabilities.

BEFORE YOU BUY

REGARDLESS OF WHETHER you've decided to use one specific curriculum or develop your own from a variety of resources, you need to plan before you buy.

First, don't dismiss learning materials that don't match your religious beliefs. Much of the prepackaged curricula and books are approached from a Christian perspective, which tends to put off those who don't subscribe to this faith. I don't suggest spending a small fortune for a complete curriculum you find offensive, but keep in mind that many of the materials do provide insight and helpful, time-tested advice.

HOW WE DID IT

I don't use resources that are designed specifically for learning disabilities. Rather, I try to use things that fit my son's learning style. We do more hands-on and games than drill work or textbooks. We get the material anywhere we can find it, or we make our own.

—TAMARA IN CALIFORNIA, PARENT TO TWO SONS, TEN AND SEVEN YEARS OLD

Look for materials and ideas that are applicable to *your* family's needs. Make your decisions by balancing the useful information with that not applicable to your life. Through the years, my family has successfully used many Christian-based books, even though our beliefs differ. In the early years, the books that never strayed far from my side were Ruth Beechick's *The Three R's*, along with Cathy Duffy's *Christian Home Educators' Curriculum Manual: Elementary Grades* and the Moore's books on delayed academics, *Better Late Than Early* and *School Can Wait*. Learn to take what you need and ignore what doesn't apply to you.

Next, resist the urge to buy whatever catches your eye. Everything at homeschool conferences, curriculum fairs, and learning supply stores tends to look wonderful! You just know that your child will adore this book and that kit. Chances are, *you're* the one who loves it. Your child, on the other hand, prefers to hide the product in the far reaches of a rarely used closet, hoping it never again sees the light of day—at least not until it reaches the "used" table at your local support group curriculum fair.

> Resist the urge to buy whatever catches your eye. Everything at homeschool conferences, curriculum fairs, and learning supply stores tends to look wonderful!

In addition, consider purchasing used materials and curricula. Homeschool curriculum fairs are a popular venue; most of them take place in June, at the end of the academic year. Other learning materials are available throughout the year through local support group sales, library book sales, and a variety of online sites. Even many school districts will sell or giveaway used textbooks.

Prospective homeschooling families sometimes express a desire to continue using materials and services from the public schools. After all, they pay taxes, which fund local schools, yet their children—especially those who have already been receiving special services—aren't using the schools. The least that parents hope for is to continue receiving some assistance while assuming the main responsibility for educating their children. Homeschooling parents are resourceful in finding learning materials, and many have used this skill to obtain or retain public school special education services.

SIMPLE STARTING POINTS

+   *Start with the library.* Get a library card for each of your children and assist them in finding topics of personal interest.

+   *Request materials catalogs from various companies or view their products online.* So much is available to homeschoolers that the selections can be overwhelming. Research the materials thoroughly and comparison-shop for the best prices.

+   *Join e-mail lists specific to a certain curriculum.* If you're interested in using a particular program, but you still want more information, many questions can be answered on e-mail lists by families currently using the curriculum. Inquire on your homeschooling special needs lists, too.

RESOURCES

College and Work

Books

Cohen, Cafi. *Homeschoolers' College Admission Handbook.* Prima Publishing, 2000.

Frances, Tarin. *Magical Quest: Creating Career Success.* Love Seeker Press, 1999.

Meyer, Roger N. *Asperger Syndrome: Employment Workbook.* Jessica Kingsley Publishers, 2001.

Mooney, Jonathan, and David Cole. *Learning Outside the Lines: Two Ivy League Students with Learning Disabilities and ADHD Give You the Tools for Academic Success and Educational Revolution.* Simon & Schuster, 2000.

Strichart, Stephen S., and Charles T. Mangrum II (eds.). *Peterson's Colleges with Programs for Students with Learning Disabilities or Attention Deficit Disorder.* Petersons Guides, 2000.

Conference Locators

A to Z Home's Cool Events Calendar: www.gomilpitas.com/home schooling/calendar/events.htm

Homeschooling Conferences by State: www.sound.net/~ejcol/confer .html

NHEN Events and Conferences: www.nhen.org/cal/

Curriculum

Alpha Omega Publications, 300 N. McKemy Avenue, Chandler, AZ 85226, 800-622-3070, www.home-schooling.com

Calvert School, 105 Tuscany Road, Baltimore, MD 21210, 410-243-6030, www.calvertschool.org

Christian Liberty Press, 502 W. Euclid Avenue, Department G, Arlington Heights, IL 60004, 800-832-2741, www.homeschools.org

Clonlara School, 1289 Jewett Street, Ann Arbor, MI 48104, 313-769-4515, www.clonlara.org

Five in a Row, P.O. Box 707, Grandview, MO 64030-0707, 816-246-9252, www.fiveinarow.com

KONOS, P.O. Box 250, Anna, TX 75409, 972-924-2712, www .konos.com

Oak Meadow School, P.O. Box 740, Putney, VT 05346, 802-387-2021, www.oakmeadow.com

Robinson Curriculum, Oregon Institute of Science and Medicine, 2251 Dick George Road, Cave Junction, OR 97523, 248-740-2746, www.robinsoncurriculum.com

Sonlight Curriculum, 8042 South Grant Way, Littleton, CO 80122-2705, 303-730-6292, www.sonlight.com

Web Sites

Cafi Cohen's Homeschool Teens and College: www.homeschool teenscollege.net

Gifted and Special Education Lesson Plans and Resources: www .cloudnet.com/~edrbsass/edexc.htm

Early Childhood Education

Books

Derman-Sparks, Louise. *Anti-Bias Curriculum: Tools for Empowering Young Children.* National Association for the Education of Young Children, 1989.

Kealoha, Anna. *Trust the Children: A Manual and Activity Guide for Homeschooling and Alternative Learning.* Celestial Arts Publishing, 1995. (Out of print, but may be available at used curriculum or online sales.)

Catalogs

Confetti Entertainment Company, 11641 Valley Spring Lane, #207, Studio City, CA 91604, 800-797-1050, www.confettibooks 4kids.com

Discount School Supply, P.O. Box 7636, Spreckels, CA 93962-7636, 800-627-2829, www.earlychildhood.com

Special Kids Videos, P.O. Box 462, Muskego, WI 53150, 800-543-7153, www.specialkids1.com

Fine Arts

Drawing on the Right Side of the Brain, 1158 26th Street, PMB 530, Santa Monica, CA 90403, 888-372-9101, www.drawright .com

Fascinating Folds (Origami), P.O. Box 10070, Glendale, AZ 85318, 888-968-2418, www.fascinating-folds.com

KidsArt Art Teaching Supplies, Box 274, Mount Shasta, CA 96067, 530-926-5076, www.kidsart.com

Lark in the Morning, P.O. Box 799, Fort Bragg, CA 95437, 707-964-5569, www.larkinam.com

Music for Little People, P.O. Box 1460, Redway, CA 95560-1460, 707-923-3991, www.mflp.com

NASCO Art Supplies, P.O. Box 901, Fort Atkinson, WI 53538-0901, or P.O. Box 3837, Modesto, CA 95352-3837, 800-558-9595, www.enasco.com

Suzuki Music Corporation, P.O. Box 261030, San Diego, CA 92196, 800-854-1594, www.suzukimusic.com

Foreign Languages

Audio Forum, 96 Broad Street, Guilford, CT 06437, 800-243-1234, www.audioforum.com

Bueno Books, 914 Pine Drive, Caldwell, TX 77836, 800-431-1579, BuenoBooks.tripod.com

Lily's World (ASL), 877-772-5459, www.lilysworld.com

Power-Glide Language Courses, 1682 W. 820 North, Provo, UT 84601, 800-596-0910, www.power-glide.com

Full Service Suppliers

American Homeschool Publishing, 5310 Affinity Court, Centreville, VA 20120, 800-684-2121, www.ahsp.com

Chinaberry Books, 2780 Via Orange Way, Suite B, Spring Valley, CA 91978, 619-670-5200, www.chinaberry.com

Christian Book Distributors, P.O. Box 7000, Peabody, MA 01961-7000, 800-247-4784, www.Christianbook.com

Dorling Kindersley Publishing, 95 Madison Avenue, New York, NY 10016, 212-213-4800, usstore.dk.com

The Education Connection, P.O. Box 910367, St. George, UT 84791, 435-656-0112, www.educationconnection.com

ESP Publishers (K–7 Super Yearbooks), 1212 N. 39th Street, Suite 444, Tampa, FL 33605, 800-643-0280, www.espbooks.com

Excellence in Education, 2640 S. Myrtle Avenue, Unit A-7, Monrovia, CA 91016, 626-821-0025, www.excellenceineducation.com

F.U.N. Books, 1688 Belhaven Wood Court, Pasadena, MD 21122, 410-360-7330, www.fun-books.com

Greenleaf Press, 3761 Hwy 109 North, Lebanon, TN 37087, 800-311-1508, www.greenleafpress.com

Michael Olaf's Essential Montessori, P.O. Box 1162, Arcata, CA 95521, 707-826-1162 or 800-429-8877

Moore Foundation, Box 1, Camus, WA 98607, 206-835-2736, www.moorefoundation.com

Poster Education, Box 8696, Asheville, NC 28814, 800-858-0969, www.postereducation.com

Rainbow Re-source Center, Route 1 Box 159A, Toulon, IL 61483, 888-841-3456, www.rainbowresource.com

Remedia Publications, 15887 North 76th Street, Suite 120, Scottsdale, AZ 85260, 800-826-4740 or 480-661-9900, www.rempub.com

Shekinah Curriculum Cellar, 101 Meador Road, Kilgore, TX 75662, 903-643-2760, www.shekinahcc.com

Timberdoodle Company, East 1510 Spencer Lake Road, Shelton, WA 98584, 360-426-0672, www.Timberdoodle.com

Usborne Books, Educational Development Corporation, 10302 E. 55th Place, Tulsa, OK 74146-6515, 800-475-4522, www.ubah.com/cat_ubah/cat-search.asp

Organizations

National Association for the Education of Young Children (NAEYC), 1509 16th Street NW, Washington, DC 20036, www.naeyc.org

Language Arts

Books

Andreola, Karen. *Simply Grammar: An Illustrated Primer*. Charlotte Mason Research & Supply Company, 1993.

Cheaney, Janie B. *Wordsmith* writing series. Common Sense Press.

Goldberg, Natalie. *Writing Down the Bones: Freeing the Writer Within*. Shambhala, 1986.

O'Conner, Patricia T. *Woe Is I: The Grammarphobe's Guide to Better English in Plain English*. Grosset/Putnam Books, 1996.

Root, Betty. *Help Your Child Learn to Read*. Usborne, 1989.

Spalding, Romalda Bishop. *The Writing Road to Reading: The Spalding Method of Phonics for Teaching Speech, Writing and Reading*. Quill, 1990.

Catalogs

Alpha-Phonics, Paradigm Publishing, Department G, P.O. Box 45161, Boise, ID 83711-5161, 208-322-4440, www.howtotutor.com

Castlemoyle Books *(Spelling Power),* The Hotel Revere Building, P.O. Box 520, Pomeroy, WA 99347-0520, 509-843-5009, www.castlemoyle.com

Common Sense Press (LLATL), 8786 Highway 21, Melrose, FL 32666, 352-475-5757, www.commonsensepress.com

Fireside Games, P.O. Box 82995, Portland, OR 97282-0095, 503-231-8990 or 800-414-8990

Handwriting Without Tears, Jan Olsen, OTR, 8802 Quiet Stream Court, Potomac, MD 20854, 301-983-8409, www.hwtears.com

National Writing Institute, 624 W. University, #248, Denton, TX 76201, 800-688-5375, www.writingstrands.com

Pecci Reading Method Educational Publishers, 440 Davis Court, #405, San Francisco, CA 94111, 415-391-8579, www.OnlineReadingTeacher.com

The Riggs Institute *(Writing Road to Reading)*, 4185 SW 102nd Avenue, Beaverton, OR 97005, 503-646-9459, www.riggsinst.org

Total Language Plus, P.O. Box 12622, Olympia, WA 98508, 360-754-3660, www.totallanguageplus.com

The Write Source, P.O. Box 460, Burlington, WI 53105, 262-763-8258, www.thewritesource.com/index2.htm

Math

Books

Burns, Marilyn. *The Book of Think: Or How to Solve a Problem Twice Your Size.* Little, Brown and Company, 1976.

Burns, Marilyn. *The I Hate Mathematics! Book.* Little, Brown and Company, 1976.

Burns, Marilyn. *Math for Smarty Pants.* Little, Brown and Company, 1982.

Enzensberger, Hans Magnus. *The Number Devil.* Metropolitan Books, 1998.

Gonick, Larry, and Woollcott Smith. *The Cartoon Guide to Statistics.* HarperCollins, 1994.

Jacobs, Harold. *Mathematics: A Human Endeavor: A Book for Those Who Think They Don't Like the Subject.* W. H. Freeman, 1994.

Mosley, Frances, and Susan Meredith. *Help Your Child Learn Number Skills.* Usborne, 1989.

Slavin, Steve. *All the Math You'll Ever Need: A Self-Teaching Guide, Revised Edition.* John Wiley & Sons, 1999.

Stenmark, Jean, Grace Coates, and Brian Gothberg. *Family Math for Young Children: Comparing.* University of California Press/Equals, 1999.

Stenmark, Jean, Virginia Thompson, Ruth Cossey, and Marilyn Hill. *Family Math.* University of California Press/Equals, 1996.

Thompson, Virginia, and Ann Humphrey. *Family Math: The Middle School Years, Algebraic Reasoning and Number Sense.* University of California Press/Equals, 1998.

Catalogs

Activity Resources, P.O. Box 4875, Hayward, CA 94541, 510-782-1300, www.activityresources.com

Brain Builder Software for Math, Sheppard Software, Suite 623, Pavilion, Jenkintown, PA 19046, 800-999-2734, www.sheppard software.com

Equals/University of California Press, Lawrence Hall of Science, University of California, Berkeley, CA 94720-5200, 510-642-1823 (programs) or 800-897-5036 (books), www.lhs.berkeley .edu/equals/

ETA/Cuisenaire, 500 Greenview Court, Vernon Hills, IL 60061, 800-445-5985, www.etacuisenaire.com/index.htm

Making Math Meaningful, Cornerstone Curriculum Project, 2006 Flat Creek, Richardson, TX 75080, 972-235-5149, www .CornerstoneCurriculum.com

Math-U-See, 1378 River Road, Drumore, PA 17518-9760, 888-854-6284, www.mathusee.com

Moving with Math, 4850 Park Glen Road, Minneapolis, MN 55416, 800-852-2435, www.movingwithmath.com/

Saxon Publishers, 1320 W. Lindsey, Norman, OK 73069, 800-284-7019, www.saxonpub.com

Singapore Math, 19363 Willamette Drive, #237, West Linn, OR 97068, 503-727-5473, www.singaporemath.com

Multiple Intelligences and Critical Thinking

Books

Black, Howard, and Sandra Park. *Building Thinking Skills Books 1–3* series. Critical Thinking Press, 1984, 1985.

Catalogs

Advanced Brain Technologies, 2380 Washington Boulevard, Suite 270, Ogden, UT 84401, 801-622-5676, www.advancedbrain.com

Critical Thinking Press and Software, P.O. Box 448, Pacific Grove, CA 93950, 408-375-0448 or 800-458-4849, www.criticalthinking .com

Science

Books

Carnegie Library of Pittsburgh. *The Handy Science Answer Book*. Visible Ink Press, 1994.

Gonick, Larry. *The Cartoon Guide to Physics*. Harper Perennial Library, 1992.

Gonick, Larry, and Alice Outwater. *The Cartoon Guide to the Environment*. HarperCollins, 1996.

Gonick, Larry, and Mark Wheelis. *The Cartoon Guide to Genetics*. Harper Perennial Library, 1991.

Lach, William (ed.). *DK Ultimate Visual Dictionary of Science*. Dorling Kindersley, 1998.

Lyons, Walt A. *The Handy Weather Answer Book*. Visible Ink Press, 1997.

Catalogs

Acorn Naturalists, 17821 East 17th Street, #103, Tustin, CA 92780, 800-422-8886 or 714-838-4888, www.acornnaturalists.com

American Science and Surplus, 3605 Howard Street, Skokie, IL 60076, 847-982-0870, www.sciplus.com

Ampersand Press, 750 Lake Street, Port Townsend, WA 98368, 800-624-4263, www.ampersandpress.com

Carolina Biological Supply Company, 2700 York Road, Burlington, NC 27215-3398, 800-334-5551, www.carolina.com

Edmund Scientific's Scientics, 60 Pierce Avenue, Tonawanda, NY 14150-6711, 800-728-6999, www.scienctificsonline.com

Flowerfield Enterprises, 10332 Shaver Road, Kalamazoo, MI 49024, 616-327-0108, www.wormwoman.com

Gardens for Growing People, P.O. Box 630, Point Reyes, CA 94956, 415-663-9433, www.svn.net/growpepl

Insect Lore, P.O. Box 1535, Shafter, CA 93263, 800-548-3284, www.insectlore.com

Let's Get Growing, 800-408-1868, www.letsgetgrowing.com

Magiscope/Brock Optical, 414 Lake Howell Road, Maitland, FL 32751, 800-780-9111, www.magiscope.com

NASCO Science, P.O. Box 901, Fort Atkinson, WI 53538-0901, or P.O. Box 3837, Modesto, CA 95352-3837, 800-558-9595, www.enasco.com

Ring-of-Fire, P.O. Box 489, Scio, OR 97374, 888-785-5439, www.sciencekitsforkids.com

Tri-Ess Sciences, 1020 W. Chestnut Street, Burbank, CA 91506, 818-848-7838, www-tri-essciences.com

Social Studies

Books

Gonick, Larry. *The Cartoon History of the United States.* Harper-Collins, 1991.

Gonick, Larry. *The Cartoon History of the Universe I: Volumes 1–7.* Doubleday Books, 1991.

Gonick, Larry. *The Cartoon History of the Universe II: From the Springtime of China to the Fall of Rome, Volumes 8–13.* Doubleday Books, 1994.

Hakim, Joy. *History of Us,* 2nd ed. Oxford Press, 1999.

Hopkins, Daniel J. (ed.). *Merriam Webster's Geographical Dictionary,* 3rd ed. Merriam Webster Publishers, 1997.

James, Peter, and Nick Thorpe. *Ancient Inventions.* Ballantine Books, 1994.

Loewen, James W. *Lies Across America: What Our Historic Sites Get Wrong.* The New Press, 1999.

Loewen, James W. *Lies My Teacher Told Me: Everything Your American History Textbook Got Wrong.* Simon & Schuster/Touchstone, 1996.

Macaulay, David. *The New Way Things Work.* Houghton Mifflin, 1998.

Zinn, Howard. *A People's History of the United States: 1492–Present.* Harper Perennial, 1995.

Catalogs

Asian American Curriculum Project (AACP), 83 37th Avenue, San Mateo, CA 94403, 650-357-1088 or 800-874-2242, www .asianamericanbooks.com

Bluestocking Press, P.O. Box 2030, Shingle Springs, CA 95682-2030, 800-959-8586, www.BluestockingPress.com

The Bookhandler, 3597 Lomacitas Lane, Bonita, CA 91902, 619-472-0471, bookhandler.com/

Boomerang!, P.O. Box 261, LaHonda, CA 94020, 800-333-7858, www.boomkids.com

California Books and More, 714 East Florence Avenue, Inglewood, CA 90301, 310-674-2400, email: californiabooks@mindspring.com

Cobblestone Publishing, 30 Grove Street, Suite C, Peterborough, NH 03458, 800-821-0115, www.cobblestonepub.com

Confetti Entertainment, 11641 Valley Spring Lane, #207, Studio City, CA 91604, 800-797-1050, www.confettibooks4kids.com/

Discovery Enterprises, 31 Laurelwood Drive, Carlisle, MA 01741, 800-729-1720, www.ugrr.org/books/discover.html

Heritage Key, 6102 E. Mescal, Scottsdale, AZ 85254, 480-483-3313

Knowledge Unlimited, P.O. Box 52, Madison, WI 53701-0052, 800-356-2303, www.ku.com

Mountain Press, P.O. Box 2399, Missoula, MT 59806, 800-234-5308 or 406-728-1900, www.mountainpresspublish.com

Nana's Book Warehouse, 848 Heber Avenue, Calexico, CA 92231, 800-737-NANA, www.nanasbookwarehouse.com

Our Land Publications, 4861 Chino Avenue, Chino, CA 91710-5132, 800-777-5292, www.ourlandofliberty.com/

Shen's Books, 40951 Fremont Boulevard, Fremont, CA 94538, 800-456-6660, www.shens.com

Women's History Project Catalog, 3343 Industrial Drive, Suite 4, Santa Rosa, CA 95403, 707-636-2888, www.nwhp.org/

Teaching Resources

Books

Beechick, Ruth. *The Three R's: A Home Start in Reading, an Easy Start in Arithmetic, and a Strong Start in Language (K–3)*. Arrow Press, 1991.

Beechick, Ruth. *You Can Teach Your Child Successfully (4–8)*. Arrow Press, 1992.

Duffy, Cathy. *Christian Home Educators' Curriculum Manual: Elementary Grades (K–6)*. Grove Publishing, 2000.

Duffy, Cathy. *Christian Home Educators' Curriculum Manual: Junior/Senior High (7–12)*. Grove Publishing, 2000.

Herzog, Joyce. *Choosing and Using Curriculum for Your Special Child*. Greenleaf Press, 1996.

Herzog, Joyce. *Learning in Spite of Labels*. Greenleaf Press, 1994.

Hirsch Jr., E.D. *Cultural Literacy: What Every American Needs to Know*. Vintage Books, 1988.

Hirsch Jr., E.D. *A First Dictionary of Cultural Literacy: What Our Children Need to Know*, 2nd ed. Mariner Books, 1996.

Hirsch Jr., E.D., Joseph Kett, and James Trefil (eds.). *Dictionary of Cultural Literacy*, 2nd ed. Houghton Mifflin, 1993.

Holdren, John, and E.D. Hirsch Jr. (eds.). *Books to Build On: A Grade-by-Grade Resource Guide for Parents and Teachers*. Delta, 1996.

Sutton, Joe P. *Strategies for the Struggling Learners: A Guide for the Teaching Parent*. Exceptional Diagnostics, 1997.

Catalogs

Action Publishing, P.O. Box 391, Glendale, CA 91209, 800-644-2665, www.actionpublishing.com

Core Knowledge Foundation, 801 East High Street, Charlottesville, VA 22902, 800-238-3233, www.coreknowledge.org

Design-a-Study, 408 Victoria Avenue, Wilmington, DE 19804-2124, 302-998-3889, www.designastudy.com/

Exceptional Diagnostics, 220 Douglas Drive, Simpsonville, SC 29681, 864-967-4729, www.edtesting.com

Grove Publishing, 16172 Huxley Circle, Westminster, CA 92683, 714-841-1220, www.grovepublishing.com

Joyce Herzog's Learning Products and Services, 1500 Albany Street, Schenectady, NY 12304, 800-745-8212, www.joyceherzog.com

Rudolf Steiner College, 9200 Fair Oaks Boulevard, Fair Oaks, CA 95628, 916-961-8729, www.steinercollege.com

Places to Buy Books

American Bookseller's Association (ABA), www.booksense.com

Quality Paperback Book Club (QPBC), Customer Service Center, Indianapolis, IN 46206-6400, 717-918-2665, www.qpb.com

Used Materials

Homeschooler's Curriculum Swap: theswap.com/toc.html

Places to Buy and Sell Used Curriculum: homeschooling.about.com/cs/usedcurriculum/

Second Harvest Curriculum, 43668 355th Avenue, Humphrey, NE 68642, www.usedhomeschoolbooks.com/index.htm

Web Sites

Arts and Entertainment Channel (A&E): www.AandE.com/class/

Discovery Channel Lesson Plans: www.school.discovery.com/lesson plans

History Channel: www.historychannel.com/classroom/index.html

How Stuff Works—Learn How Everything Works!: www.howstuff
works.com

Jet Propulsion Laboratory (JPL): www.jpl.nasa.gov

PBS: www.pbs.org/teachersource/

Smithsonian: www.smithsonianstore.com (866-538-6195)

World Book Course of Study: www.worldbook.com/ptrc/html
/curr.htm

10

HOMESCHOOLERS AND SCHOOL-PROVIDED SPECIAL NEEDS PROGRAMS

In This Chapter

✦ Milestones in special education

✦ Opting out of services

✦ Needed services never materialized

✦ Public school services for homeschooled children

✦ Do public school IEPs and homeschooling mix?

✦ Developing your own IEP for homeschooling

© EyeWire

$\mathcal{M}$ANY PARENTS WHO are dissatisfied with the day-to-day public education of their special needs children wouldn't hesitate to remove them from school and educate at home, except for one crucial aspect—services. Parents are frequently apprehensive about finding and paying for replacement services once the child leaves the public special education program.

To be sure, some parents don't think twice about losing public school services when they homeschool. Many say that their children were receiving substandard assistance, and anything they could give their children at home could only be better. Other parents see limited results from their children's therapeutic school services, but are reluctant to give up free services provided by certified teachers. These parents fear that the elimination of services could cause irreparable harm to their children. Many parents feel that good parenting alone doesn't qualify them to work with their special needs children.

Many parents have successfully found assistance outside of the public setting. Others have managed to hold onto a minimum of school services. But why have we become so dependent upon special education services for our differently abled children? It's interesting to note that until fairly recently, school services for differently abled children were virtually nonexistent. During the mid- to late-1800s, educational reformers advocated schooling deaf, blind, and physically or emotionally impaired children. However, this movement was short lived, and by the turn of the century, it was felt that these children were not educable. Many such children were not permitted to even attend school. If they were allowed to, placement was in segregated classrooms away from "normal" youth. Institutions where differently abled children received limited or no treatment also flourished. Families were generally embarrassed by their "defective" offspring and "hid" them in asylums. Through the first half of the twentieth century, the treatments of choice for the impaired (including children) were electronic convulsive therapy (ECT) and psychosurgery (the lobotomy). It wasn't until the 1950s when families began advocating humane services and living conditions for their differently abled young. This movement was helped tremendously when prominent individuals publicly discussed their own "different" children—paving the way toward public acceptance or, at least, tolerance.

Despite a century of "progress," differently abled children are still referred to by less-than-flattering terms, and some continue to be housed in institutions where they must submit to forced and, at times, inhumane treatment. Families should not willingly accept substandard public school services that mirror the conditions of the past.

MILESTONES IN SPECIAL EDUCATION

IN 1917, THE Connecticut Asylum for the Education and Instruction of Deaf and Dumb Persons opened as the first permanent school to specifically address the needs of disabled (in this case, deaf) children. Over the next few years, similar schools for deaf students opened in New York and Pennsylvania.

By the 1850s, the medical model had replaced the previously used educational model, and the headmaster of a Pennsylvania asylum school had taken to referring to his charges as "inmates" rather than "students."

Mental health organizations came to life in the 1890s with the establishment of the Medical Officers of American Institutions for Idiotic and Feeble-minded People. By 1896, the United States' first public special education class opened in Rhode Island. The first compulsory attendance laws, however, were not initiated until 1852 in Massachusetts. An 1894 survey of public schools in California reported that 9 percent of the pupils were "mentally dull," while 2 percent were classified as "feeble-minded." Of the 10,842 students attending California schools at the time, 6 percent were deemed "imbeciles or idiots." The classifications for special education have changed through the years, while its student population has dropped to 9 percent of the 6,050,895 children currently enrolled in California public schools.

The American Speech-Language-Hearing Association (ASHA), a private association, was organized in 1925. In 1946, the federal government founded the National Institute of Mental Health (NIMH). The American Psychiatric Association published its first Diagnostic and Statistical Manual (DSM) in 1952, detailing the various mental

> In the 1850s, the headmaster of a Pennsylvania asylum school had taken to referring to his charges as "inmates" rather than "students."

health disorders. All three entities still exist, and the psychiatric organization published the fourth edition of DSM in 1994.

In 1953, entertainer Dale Evans Rogers wrote *Angel Unaware*, a book about her Down's syndrome child. She advocated keeping children with disabilities at home, rather than institutionalizing them, which was still the norm at the time.

The implementation of special education and civil rights laws slowly evolved through the decades until reaching our current protections for children with special needs.

Legislative Initiatives

In 1975, Congress passed the Educational for All Handicapped Children Act, a public law (PL 94-142). Congress reauthorized the law in 1997 as the Individuals with Disabilities Education Act (IDEA). The intent of both PL 94-142 and IDEA has been to provide federal funding to state and local school districts for the education of children between the ages of three and twenty-one who have physical, learning, or mental disabilities. Under IDEA and its predecessor, all qualifying children must receive a free, appropriate public education (FAPE). This means that children are entitled to special education services and accommodations at no cost to their parents. The children are to be granted these services within the least restrictive environment (LRE) available.

IDEA is buttressed by Section 504 of the Rehabilitation Act of 1973 and Title II of the Americans with Disabilities Act (ADA).

Section 504

If a child is disabled but doesn't qualify for special education, he is still protected under Section 504 of the Rehabilitation Act of 1973. This is a civil rights law providing equal access to public school buildings, as well as providing for the child who requires classroom modifications in order to learn (without supplying funds from

IDEA). Those who use Section 504 protections don't have as many rights as those receiving services under IDEA. However, many children enrolled in public schools have their needs accommodated in various ways, such as untimed proctored testing in a quiet environment, rather than in the classroom.

Americans with Disabilities Act

The U.S. Congress passed the Americans with Disabilities Act (ADA) of 1990 to prevent discrimination against individuals with physical or mental disabilities. The law evoked a groundswell of advocacy toward full inclusion of disabled children in regular classroom settings (as opposed to special classes). The issues surrounding inclusion are beyond the scope of this book. One aspect of this movement, however, has affected the education of many children who have been removed from school and are now educated at home. The placement of severely disabled children with those possessing only mild to moderate difficulties has caused many parents of the latter group to realize that their children's abilities were declining— possibly as a result of modeling behaviors of the lower-functioning children. Louisiana homeschool parent Victoria cites this as one of her reasons for homeschooling. She's found that one of the positive effects of educating her ADHD thirteen-year-old son at home has been his ability to "get together with 'regular' kids more and away from the bad habits and patterns of severely disturbed kids."

Individualized Education Plans

To qualify for services under IDEA, an individualized education plan (IEP) must be formulated for the child in need. The IEP is the cornerstone of special education law; it is the blueprint outlining a student's academic or behavioral needs and the proposed methods of remediation. A sample IEP is shown on page 185. The IEP team typically comprises the school's special education or resource specialist, nurse, school psychologist, counselor, parents, and the child's regular classroom teacher. School officials may try to limit or deny services. If parents anticipate such a move, they may decide to hire their own "team" of private psychologists and attorneys to act as a child advocate in the meeting. The IEP meeting participants review the child's case file, which may include standardized test scores, notes from behavioral observations, or work samples. School officials will determine the child's need and provide a written account of goals to be attained by the child within a certain time. The IEP also stipulates the type and frequency of services to be administered in order for the child's goals to be met. Every three years, IDEA requires that reevaluations be conducted, although many schools update students' IEPs annually.

OPTING OUT OF SERVICES

COUNTLESS PARENTS AND special education advocates battle regularly with school districts to enforce the services that children's IEPs state that they need. Parents frequently complain that IEPs tend to be written in vague generalities that don't address individual needs and disabilities. Others report that their children are treated with ill-defined methods, usually nothing more than a classroom serving as a holding tank for children viewed as misfits by teachers and the school staff. As a result, many parents feel no qualms in abandoning the special education services in favor of homeschooling.

> Many parents feel no qualms in abandoning the special education services in favor of homeschooling.

Lisa, the Michigan parent of an autistic daughter, scoffs at the notion of special needs programs: "My daughter's school services were a joke. The school wouldn't have allowed us to continue services once we started homeschooling, which was fine as I was not impressed with what they had to offer." Instead, Lisa has opted for alternatives outside of the school system. "I provide my daughter with direct therapy services at home under the direction of professionals at a

Sample Individualized Educational Plan

Browne Family Homeschool—Los Angeles, CA

STUDENT: <u>Malik Browne</u>   GRADE: <u>6</u>

Begin/End Dates: March 2001 to March 2002

For the Following Areas:

<u>X</u> Academic Skills   ___ Behavior/Social Emotional

___ Communication/Language   ___ Gross/Fine Motor

___ Medical/Health   ___ Self-Help

+ Current Level of Performance (Based on assessment, observation, work samples, and progress from previous IEP):

Malik is at a fifth-grade reading level with good comprehension and response to interpretive questions.

+ Annual Goal:

By March 2002, Malik will be able to read fluently from a 5.5–6.0 grade level text. He will also be able to provide oral and written answers to questions based on his reading, getting at least 8 out of 10 correct.

+ Instructional Objectives

#1. By June 2001, when given a 5.0 grade level text, Malik will read with a teacher and provide oral and written answers to questions, getting 6 out of 10 correct.

#2. By September 2001, when given a 5.0 grade level text, Malik will read fluently and provide oral and written answers to questions, getting 8 out of 10 correct.

#3. By December 2001, when given a 5.5–6.0 grade level text, Malik will read fluently and provide oral and written answers to questions, getting 6 out of 10 correct.

#4. By March 2002, when given a 5.5–6.0 grade level text, Malik will read fluently and provide oral and written answers to questions, getting 8 out of 10 correct.

rehabilitation center. They provide some treatment at the center, as well as a home therapy program so I can work with her on my own."

Linda, the mother of a daughter with Asperger's Syndrome in Northern California, exclaims, "No way did I want to keep school services! I just wanted to get away from the government-run schools!" She withdrew her daughter from public school and told the special education director of the local school district that she was enrolling her daughter in a private school and his services would no longer be needed. The private school was the homeschool that Linda had already set up for her younger child.

Some realize that their children's special education assistance could be a detriment to homeschooling and want services discontinued. Carole in Massachusetts knew that she was going to remove her son from public school, but she was cautious, not wanting repercussions from the school district over her decision to homeschool. "Before the school knew I would be homeschooling, I encouraged them to dismiss Michael from the speech and language services. They took the bait and did this." She continues, "I did this because I didn't want the public school to file an educational neglect report against us for not providing speech and language while homeschooling.

NEEDED SERVICES NEVER MATERIALIZED

ANOTHER GROUP OF parents realize that their children desperately need assistance, yet do not qualify for special education services under the federal guidelines. Because Section 504 provides limited assistance, these children are left to fend for themselves in mainstream classrooms.

"My son was evaluated for an IEP three separate times after a return from an adolescent psychiatric facility," fumes Rhonda of Michigan. "The school's special education director admitted my son would never succeed the way he was going, but still refused to give him an IEP. Apparently, his IQ measured 142, which, according to the director, disqualified him from services. I knew this was illegal, but after fighting for two years, during which time my son was suicidal and our entire family was being torn apart, I knew we had to change, so we started homeschooling."

PUBLIC SCHOOL SERVICES FOR HOMESCHOOLED CHILDREN

CAN PARENTS POSSIBLY homeschool and use public special services? In March 1999, the federal government issued new guidelines under IDEA, one of which included the removal of the requirement that schools provide a free and appropriate public education for special needs children whose parents have chosen to place them in private schools. However, many public schools will continue to provide some services to nonenrolled students. The decision rests solely on your state and local school district. Most local districts refuse to provide services to children who are not enrolled in their schools. Since federal funding to implement IDEA is limited, state and local education offices find themselves with too little money to provide special education services for too many children. Administrators frequently observe that it would be inequitable to provide for those enrolled in private schools chosen by the parents or homeschooled when the schools are not meeting the full needs of the children enrolled in public programs.

What the Law Says

In the April 2001 edition of the *California Homeschooler* (published by the Homeschool Association of California), attorney and homeschooling parent Linda Conrad-Jansen wrote: "The federal government provides funding for special education, and the states must operate within the guidelines of the United States Code (USC) and the Code of Federal Regulations (CFR). Children with disabilities enrolled in private schools are also entitled to special education services (34 CFR §300.451)." She added, "The state is not required to 'pay for the cost of education, including special education and related services, of a child with a disability at a private school or facility if that agency made a free appropriate public education available to the child and the parents elected to place the child in such private school or facility. (20 USC 1412(a)(10)(C))."

Conrad-Jansen continued, "The states have a certain amount of discretion when providing special education benefits to home-based private schools. If they argue that they offered a 'free appropriate public education' that was rejected by the parents, they are not required to offer additional services."

Although homeschoolers' prospects of receiving or continuing public school services appear grim, the door isn't completely closed and locked. "The provision of special education services by the government is a complicated legal area, full of interpretation and argument. A relatively new area, it is growing rapidly," added Conrad-Jansen in the April 2001 article. "Recent court decisions clarify the law, and more cases are under submission. If both the provision of special needs services and homeschooling independently are critical parts of your education, research all of your alternatives. On the surface, the law appears to support the denial of services if 'free appropriate public education' is available, but the law is in flux. Therefore, if the services offered by the district do not meet your child's needs, it may be worthwhile to obtain legal help to enforce your child's right to a 'free appropriate public education.' Just because a child has been determined to be a special

> Although homeschoolers' prospects of receiving or continuing public school services appear grim, the door isn't completely closed and locked.

needs child and an IEP has been prepared for her, does not mean that her family loses their constitutional right to choose the best educational alternative for the child. Parents can elect to place their child in a private school or facility (20 USC 1412 (a)(10)(C))."

It is possible, but difficult, to receive public school services for a homeschooled child. Be sure you ask yourself if it's worth fighting for services that were already not addressing your child's needs when he was in the public setting.

DO PUBLIC SCHOOL IEPS AND HOMESCHOOLING MIX?

THE 1999 UPDATE of IDEA regulations stipulates that special education children who have been placed by parents in nonpublic schools may still receive some services or consultations. However, the 1999 update has changed the terminology—an IEP can only be developed for a public school student. Private school students now receive their learning blueprint as what is called a *service plan*.

Those Who Have Kept Services

Some homeschooling parents of children with special needs have been able to work with the public schools to get the services their child needs. "The school district where our son, Zek, attended early intervention was going to let us continue with services while we homeschooled," recalls Erika in California. "He received occupational and physical therapies with sensory integration twice weekly. He also received group speech therapy three times weekly, but I eventually discontinued these services because he was getting sick so much and missing most of the sessions. We then moved to a new school district where Zek received a very thorough triennial evaluation. The speech pathologist offered services for Zek individually, as well on a consultation basis. We chose the latter because Zek's speech was only six months behind his chronological age of six years old at that point."

Kerri of South Dakota devised an unusual but highly workable plan for her developmentally delayed son. "It was questionable if our son was ready for kindergarten," she recalls. "So our developmental pediatrician recommended we 'dual enroll' him. The plan was that our son would attend mornings at the public school's early childhood program for delayed kids, as well as afternoon kindergarten at a small private Lutheran school." The private school didn't offer the

HOW WE DID IT

When we adopted Rosie, we knew that she had a cleft lip and palate. Within weeks of her arrival at the age of nine months, she had the lip closure done, and six months later, the palate. By nineteen months of age, Rosie was in speech therapy twice a week through California Children's Services. We met with the school district for an Individualized Educational Plan (IEP) and speech services when Rosie turned three. She had speech therapy twice a week for half an hour for the next three years, and then went to once a week for forty-five minutes. Rosie was homeschooled from kindergarten through the beginning of sixth grade.

We kept our public school services when Rosie entered sixth grade at a local private school. When Rosie's vision began to deteriorate, we asked for a vision consult and received help from the district's vision specialist for two years until Rosie had successful corneal transplants and could see well again.

A consult is an advising meeting where the speech (or other) therapist assesses the child and discusses with the parent what needs work. But the therapist doesn't see the child weekly or do the actual sessions. It helps if the parent knows what goals the child has.

needed therapies, but even if it had, Kerri's family couldn't afford the full-time tuition. So this plan provided her son with the needed speech and physical therapies through the public school, while receiving a part-time private school education.

As it came time to enroll Kerri's son in the first grade at the public school, however, she realized his class had twenty-eight kids in it. She felt he wouldn't do well in such a large setting. They reached a workable solution by deciding to homeschool, while taking him to public school daily for the resource room and his therapies.

Kerri's son is now ten years old and has been homeschooled for four years. "After the first year, he no longer qualified for physical

Although consultations are on an as-needed basis, our district allows only four meetings in a calendar year. By the time Rosie entered high school, the laws regarding provision of services by public school special education departments to parentally placed private school pupils had changed. This change coincided with the retirement of our wonderful kid-advocate speech therapist. I called the district office and asked for consultation four times a year. Since Rosie was continuing to have staged craniofacial procedures, we knew that she would need additional speech therapy to cope with the new, improved equipment. I discussed Rosie's situation with the district head of special education and requested services on a consultation basis.

We were granted the consultation basis, and can see the speech therapist up to four times per school year. Since Rosie has an open IEP, we are using it. The current speech therapist actually worked with Rosie when she was four years old, so it's a nice reunion for them. If it turns out that Rosie needs further help, I will request it, but I recognize that the school district may refuse.

—CAROL EDSON, CALIFORNIA

therapy and special education," she says. "But the local school was cooperative and willing to work with us. Our son still qualifies and has been receiving speech therapy for the past four years."

Some public school assistance arrives as an unexpected and very welcome gift. "Actually, at the time my son left school, I wanted to cut all ties with the public schools," recalls Jennifer in California. "But the school speech therapist called and offered services even though we were homeschooling. I accepted because we've been on a waiting list for private speech for the past seven months."

The school was to prove even more cooperative with Jennifer and her son, JR. A new IEP needed to be scheduled, and the resource specialist had initially told Jennifer he felt it would be necessary for her son to attend daily resource classes. However, after the assessment and consultations with the speech therapist and a previous teacher who had kept up with JR's progress, the resource specialist made an unusual determination. Jennifer explains, "The resource specialist fully supports homeschooling after realizing that JR learns best at home. I now have an IEP that states homeschooling is the best placement for him!"

Jennifer attributes this decision to JR exhibiting a newly acquired leadership role in speech, when the year before he hadn't wanted to participate in speech therapy at all. Another recent addition to JR's growing repertoire of skills is his ability to finish what he starts.

DEVELOPING YOUR OWN IEP FOR HOMESCHOOLING

ONE OF THE benefits of homeschooling is that it is very much an individualized education plan regardless of your child's disability or whether she even has any learning problems. Homeschooling has the potential to speak to each child's individual needs.

Even if you are not going to use public school services, you can still develop your own learning plans. Some homeschoolers work with special education teachers, therapists, or other practitioners. Many more develop learning plans, formal or informal, on their own.

"A special needs teacher helps me write up some goals for each year," says Deborah of Pennsylvania. "We work on those goals throughout the year. My son learns so slowly that we work on the same skills many times. I use his 'mistakes' to develop lessons," she adds. "For example, he'll say 'Tie my shoe,' but his speech is so garbled he has to repeat it a few times for me to understand. So I take that sentence and copy it on paper, and we practice the words and phrases that he is trying to communicate."

> Even if you are not going to use public school services, you can still develop your own learning plans.

Components of a Learning Plan

Numerous books, Web sites, and workshops offer assistance in developing IEPs. Although most are directed toward the child in public school, many of the suggestions can be applied to homeschooled children as well.

A good learning plan consists of the following.

Identification of Need

What are your child's learning or behavior difficulties? Write a description of them. This should be based on subjective information (such as parent or classroom observations) and objective data (such as standardized tests and assessments). Keep in mind that the opinion of a teacher, psychologist, or doctor is subjective unless it can be supported with documentation (medical and other valid screening measures).

Current Level

What is your child's present level of performance? If your learning plan is informal, it's preferable to stick with your subjective assessment. For example, you and your daughter read together daily, and although she's eager and loves it, she just doesn't seem to be showing interest in reading to herself. To assess this situation, use both your subjective and objective data. Look at what you have observed during your reading sessions (subjective), as well as at the scores from a standardized reading assessment (objective), to determine if she is definitely delayed.

Goals

What specific tasks or behaviors do you want to accomplish? Although it's best to focus on only a few goals at a time, you'll also want to determine some long-term goals for your child. In the previous example, your long-term goal would be for your daughter to read a book to herself without adult assistance. Her short-term goals might be to sound out words or develop word identification skills. These short-term goals are the steps she would take to reach the ultimate goal of reading to herself.

Objectives

What specific interventions will you use to reach the goals? For example, you realize that your son and phonics are not a good fit and that it would be easier for him to learn to read using a different method. The two of you decide to write words of household items (lamp, rug, window) on cards that you affix to the respective items. Through daily interaction with the words, your son learns to identify them by sight without the corresponding item. You continue this process by constantly adding new words.

Progress

How are you going to know that your child has accomplished the goals? If you're following a formal learning plan approach, your child's progress will be measured by the results of additional standardized tests. Those using more subjective assessment criteria (a parent's intuition) will just know that a child has met the goals.

Developing and working on educational or behavioral goals may sound like a daunting task to the new homeschooling parent, but the possibilities are endless. Many families rely on the assistance of medical and mental health professionals to come up with goals, while others do it on their own, with assistance from other parents and resource materials.

SIMPLE STARTING POINTS

✦ *Contact your state homeschooling organization for information on public school services for homeschooled children.* You're probably not the first homeschooler in the state seeking public services, and a state organization would know how those before you have fared.

✦ *Keep a journal of your child's learning experiences.* Even if you're not interested in developing a learning plan, it's so helpful to keep track of what your child has accomplished, her favorite books and activities, and her progress.

✦ *Consider private services if you can't obtain or keep public special education.* Private services come from a variety of sources and many are surprisingly affordable. See for yourself in the next chapter.

RESOURCES

Books

Siegal, Lawrence. *The Complete IEP Guide: How to Advocate for Your Special Ed Child.* Nolo Press, 2000.

Wright, Peter W. D., and Pamela Darr. *Wrightslaw: Smart IEPs.* Harbor House Law Press, 2002.

Wright, Peter W. D., and Pamela Darr. *Wrightslaw: Special Education Law.* Harbor House Law Press, 1999.

Web Sites

Attorneys and Advocates

Association of Homeschool Attorneys: www.ahsa-usa.org

Council of Parent Attorneys and Advocates: www.copaa.net

Disability Rights Education and Defense Fund, Inc.: www.dredf.org

IDEA Practices: www.ideapractices.org

Reed Martin Special Education Law: www.reedmartin.com

National Information Center for Children and Youth with Disabilities (NICHCY): www.nichcy.org/

Special Ed Law: www.specialedlaw.net/idex.mv

Wrightslaw: www.wrightslaw.com

IEP Assistance

Rhonda Robinson's Recipe for a Homeschooled IEP: www.nathhan .com/recipeiep.htm

Service Unit 10 in Kearney, NE: www.esu10.k12.ne.us/~sped/obj /objhp.html

Special Education Goals and Objectives, Educational Service Unit 10 in Kearney, NE: www.esu10.k12.ne.us/~sped/obj/objhp.html

11

HOMESCHOOL-FRIENDLY SERVICES FOR YOUR CHILD

In This Chapter

✦ Government services

✦ Private services

✦ University clinics

✦ Intervention at home

✦ Approaches that have not worked

✦ Diagnosis by school officials

✦ Nightmares on the therapy-go-round

✦ How-to's of locating therapy

✦ Other medical professionals

© EyeWire

*I*F YOU'RE NOT able to keep your child's school services, or if you've opted out of them, you'll want to locate other sources of help. In the perfect world, you'd want to obtain the very best providers for your child, but these professionals' price tags often keep most of us at bay. Health insurance companies' resources are woefully lacking when dealing with long-term preexisting conditions, and they will not provide more than a handful of appointments with mental health professionals.

Parents are an enterprising force when it comes to locating services for their special needs children. Adding the homeschool component only makes these parents more ingenious. Special needs parents who homeschool search numerous Web sites and e-mail lists, reading about others' successful experiences that they could apply to their own children. Researchers are swamped with letters and e-mail from parents inquiring about the latest findings, possible clinical trials for new medications; some parents even travel to research facilities and hospitals far from home, searching for answers.

Homeschooling families draw from a variety of services, often combining low-cost or free agency provisions with occasional private services, while also using professional input to work with their children at home. Many therapists are more than happy to provide training to parents so they can work with their children at home.

GOVERNMENT SERVICES

GOVERNMENT-BASED SERVICES are funded by federal and state governments and are delivered at the state and county levels.

"We still see a psychiatrist because my daughter receives Social Security Insurance (SSI), so we have to show some kind of effort to take care of her disability," says Linda, a Northern California mother with an autistic daughter. Linda admits that she hates taking government services, along with the requisite hoop-jumping. She doesn't find her daughter's psychiatrist to be supportive of homeschooling. As a parent accepting public services, Linda is also wary of challenges to her decision to educate her daughter at home. She states, "All it would take to really cause problems for our family is one psychiatric report saying I'm doing the wrong thing." Linda had already dealt with the anguish of warding off the efforts of the local children's mental health program to place her daughter in a county-run program for autistic children. Linda's daughter had tried special programs, and they only seemed to worsen her condition. Homeschooling was successfully meeting the child's needs.

Other types of government-funded services are available to individuals whose onset of disabilities began before adulthood. Check with your state's office for mental health or developmental disabilities.

PRIVATE SERVICES

IT IS OFTEN necessary for families to obtain outside services for their children's needs. Because the services provided at no cost by public schools are often substandard or insufficient, parents will look to private services. This means that the services, which can be costly, are paid out-of-pocket or by the family's insurance carrier. Unfortunately, many insurance companies balk at picking up the tab for services deemed unnecessary or of a psychological nature. Homeschooling parent Erika, whose oldest son has been diagnosed with Asperger's Syndrome, has faced these concerns, "Our insurance will not cover anything because they term autism a 'mental disorder.' This categorization really needs to be changed. Autistic spectrum disorders are not mental; they are neurological."

Many other parents decide the cost is necessary, and so they tighten their budgets in other areas. Some families are fortunate enough to have flexible plans through their employers that allow them some financial relief. "To offset the cost, we declare it as a medical expense through my husband's payroll Flexible Spending Account (FSA). It doesn't exactly pay us back, but because of the nature of FSA, we get a tax-break, and, in effect, that's a 30 percent discount. My son loves OT, so it's worth it."

Even those parents whose children were previously enrolled in and receiving public school services opted for private services before deciding to homeschool. Lisa, the Michigan mother of an autistic

> Because the services provided at no cost by public schools are often substandard or insufficient, parents will look to private services.

daughter, has always preferred private services for her daughter. "I used outside services before we homeschooled, in order to have professionals who aren't accountable to the school, which was always trying to discontinue services." Lisa's daughter is a veteran of multiple therapies—speech, occupational, sensory integration, vision, challenged ski program, and an annual check by the auditory integration therapist.

UNIVERSITY CLINICS

UNIVERSITY OUTPATIENT CLINICS are useful, often overlooked, resources for low-cost, quality services. In such programs, advanced graduate students, under the supervision of licensed professionals, are the primary providers of speech, mental health, and occupational therapies. But don't view these student practitioners as completely inexperienced. Most are working toward licensing hours and can bring a fresh outlook to therapy because they are up-to-date on innovative techniques and current research findings.

University programs generally work on a sliding fee scale and are geared toward short-term therapies, with an emphasis on training the parent to work with the child at home. Attests Cherlynn, a Missouri homeschooling parent, "We used a professional speech therapist for initial assessments, then located inexpensive services from a university."

In addition to the various therapies, many university education departments offer a sliding scale for testing, assessment, and remediation services provided by teachers in training.

INTERVENTION AT HOME

FINANCIAL NECESSITY AND choice both cause many parents to provide the majority of therapeutic services at home with minimal professional intervention. Some will make use of professional services on an as-needed basis; others will schedule consulting appointments to discuss the child's progress and receive feedback.

"We are not using any services at this time," admits Erika. "We live in a district that is very low income with poor services. To pay for services on our own would be too costly."

Speech Therapy at Home

However, Erika's children are not without therapeutic resources; she has dedicated herself to working with them by using periodic professional consultations and readily available materials. "We obtained speech consultations for my son through the local school district. This allows me to set up an appointment with the school's speech therapist when I need assistance, and she tells me what I could do to work on whatever difficulty he's having. We incorporate speech or language therapy into five-minute segments throughout the day, making speech therapy a regular part of life. Also," Erika adds, "thousands of homeschooling families are using the 'Straight Talk' manuals in place of going to weekly therapy. It's not as if it's rocket science."

> Many parents make use of professional services on an as-needed basis; others schedule consulting appointments to discuss the child's progress and receive feedback.

Social Skills Training

Children develop the abilities to interact socially by observing the behaviors of adults and children around them. Gradually, children grow to understand the meaning behind such social cues as body language and facial expressions. Societal expectations of acceptable behaviors are also realized as a child matures. Yet many children with attentional and autistic spectrum differences are unable to grasp many of these social nuances. This is one of the key reasons why these children encounter so much difficulty within a school setting. An Asperger's Syndrome or ADD child simply doesn't get it when required to raise a hand to be called upon, rather than blurting out a comment or question. He doesn't understand that his myopic interest in changing weather patterns and barometric pressure sets him up to be ridiculed by peers who find his behavior and words peculiar.

Social skills training is the common method of working with children who encounter these interpersonal differences. Although school children may receive small group counseling with other similar children, or parents may seek outside assistance from a psychotherapist or other mental health professional, this is an area that is especially well-suited for home intervention.

I've worked with my son through the years on social skills, using a few key methods. When he was young, we spent a lot of time each day reading the Berenstain Bear books, which present the bear children encountering and eventually solving a variety of problems. The stories would serve as a starting point to discuss similar issues in my son's life. (Noted lecturer Carol Gray has authored books on the use of developing stories to assist individuals with social skills. Her Web site provides some basic guidelines for this invaluable tool.)

My son and I also made faces in the mirror to express how we were feeling. We used the popular "How Are You Feeling Today?" poster, which shows a wide variety of facial expressions, as our guide. This daily activity allowed my son to see what different emotions look like. He also practiced looking angry, happy, and many other emotions. During the day, we'd look at magazines or television shows, or just at people in a public place, and state what we felt their faces were conveying.

Our mainstay has been (and continues to be) generating options for various situations. In working with my son, I'll bring up a previous situation when he encountered difficulty. We'll talk through what transpired and then discuss all the alternative actions he could've used and how they could've changed a negative outcome into a positive one. When he's acted in a manner that has brought him the desired results, we discuss how different actions may have produced problems. Other times I'll present him with a hypothetical situation, or we'll rehearse what he's going to say and do in an up-coming encounter. We address these areas on a daily basis so that my son receives regular practice and input.

Working with Reading Difficulties

An unqualified favorite of many homeschooling families whose children struggle with reading is the approach developed by the Davis Dyslexia Association. Founded by Ron Davis, author of *The Gift of Dyslexia* and himself a dyslexic, the organization provides a variety of tools to assist with reading difficulties. Parents and children can participate in workshops offered by trained practitioners at the California headquarters and other sites around the world. If that's too pricey, the organization also sells a variety of books and tapes.

Louisiana parent Susan has been pleased with the services: "For my daughter's dyslexia, we are using a modified method of orientation training based on Ron Davis's book, *The Gift of Dyslexia*. We've been in contact with the Davis association, and they have helped me to develop a program that meets my daughter's needs."

Tracy in California is another parent satisfied with the approach. "I read Ron Davis's *The Gift of Dyslexia,* then researched dyslexia quite a bit on the Internet before I found a practitioner I was comfortable with. My daughter was never made to feel like she had a handicap or problem. She felt supported and strengthened during her time spent working with the program." Tracy announces, "We're working on our own now—so far, so good!"

> An unqualified favorite of many homeschooling families whose children struggle with reading is the approach developed by the Davis Dyslexia Association.

Sensory Integration

After years of battling with school officials to receive needed services, Jennifer, a California mother of five, eventually reached a breaking point. She received a flyer from the Epilepsy Foundation of Los Angeles about a program called Brain Gym that involved "integrating the brain." Her eight-year-old son had sensory integration dysfunction, so she thought the program could be beneficial. Because the schools had not been meeting her son's needs, Jennifer was compelled to take charge of his education. He started the school year in September, and Jennifer started working with her son on a daily basis. At the start of the academic year, her son was unable to write and could only recognize a handful of letters from the alphabet. Yet when he was assessed in November for his annual IEP, he quite capably printed the entire alphabet in capital letters. "At that time," Jennifer recalls, "I realized I could do more for him at home than they ever could at school."

After taking the initial Brain Gym course and purchasing a few books, Jennifer has been able to determine what work needs to be done to assist her children. "The training and books allow you to do this on your own. However," she adds, "when we are making a big shift, I can consult with my Brain Gym instructor to map out a new plan of action. She's a former special education teacher and has been incredibly supportive of homeschooling."

Jennifer admits the cost ($400.00) of the four-day, thirty-two-hour course caused her family to temporarily tighten the budget. But, she offers, "I took that class over two years ago, and my family is still reaping the benefits from it. I don't think many therapies are that affordable and effective."

Benefits of Diet Therapy

Balanced and nutritional eating habits are an accepted way to maintain optimum health. However, many individuals choose to isolate and remove one or more of the basic food groups in order to eliminate undesirable behaviors or other disturbances. Although those who are following one of the many therapeutic diets available frequently cite improvement, medical and mental health professionals

HOW WE HOMESCHOOL THERAPY

As a young child, my youngest daughter had a lot of speech impediments. A homeschooling friend lent me a book that suggested waiting until a child was seven years old before enrolling her in speech therapy. The book said that most impediments correct themselves by this age. I was a little wary since she was so unintelligible. Still, we waited until age seven, and all but one impediment disappeared. She still had a very significant lisp that made her hard to understand, so we used the book *Help Me Talk Right: How to Correct a Child's Lisp in 15 Easy Lessons,* by Mirla G. Raz. The book deals with more than the standard lisp. It includes game sheets, consumable worksheets, outlined fun lessons, and record sheets. It was rather expensive (more than $30.00), but my daughter loves working with it, and she learned how to control her lisp very quickly. When the lisp didn't totally disappear, we took her to an orthodontist on the recommendation of her dentist. While some corrective work can be done, her top and bottom teeth are so far apart that her jaw needs moving. That will likely correct the remaining difficulty she is having forming the sounds.

—TIFFANY IN CALIFORNIA, PARENT TO TWO DAUGHTERS, AGES EIGHT AND TEN YEARS OLD

tend to cast a suspicious eye toward claims of success based solely on diet change. Again, this is one of those controversial areas where parents need to determine for themselves what is or isn't appropriate.

Tammy in Alaska decided to try a dietary approach to deal with some of her autistic daughter's difficulties, which included craving foods containing milk or wheat, intolerance to the slightest amount of pain, and moods alternating between social withdrawal and overt giggling. Tammy felt that if the results were unsatisfactory after a six-month period, she could return her daughter to her previous diet. Time was the only thing they had to lose. Within two weeks, the diet showed signs of success. Tammy's daughter Pamela finally developed bladder control for the first time in her life. She had complete control within two months of trying the new diet, and a longstanding bowel disorder finally cleared up. Tammy exclaims, "For me, if that was the only benefit, the diet was well worth it!"

Pamela's elimination diet also brought behavioral benefits. She acquired pretend play skills, started speaking spontaneously (rather than speech limited to addressing her needs), learned to ask questions, became less rigid about change, and became more aware of others. "The diet has not cured Pamela," Tammy says, "but it brought her from low-functioning to high-functioning autism. I only wish we had started it when she was younger."

APPROACHES THAT HAVE NOT WORKED

AS MOST PARENTS quickly learn, some so-called therapeutic interventions do not work. Some failures are due to the various cottage industry scams guaranteeing cures for incurable disorders. Unlicensed and even licensed professionals may prey on desperate families seeking to ease their children's learning and health difficulties. I recall listening to the horror stories of learning disabled students when I worked as a counselor for a university-based program. One highly touted program made claims to eliminate dyslexia by utilizing special eyeglasses. Many students in the program flocked to this clinic to be fitted for the glasses. Initial successes disappeared within a few months, and the dissatisfied students were advised to return for new evaluations at a hefty cost.

However, most intervention failures are simply the result of a poor fit with individual children. What might work for twelve children in your online support group may not make a whit of difference in your own child.

Looking to assist her sixteen-year-old daughter's reading difficulties, Tracy in California found the first attempt at intervention to be lacking. "We used something called visual therapy for a while. The idea is that the eyes are not coordinated with the brain properly, so you do exercises to strengthen the eyes and muscles. It was a waste of time and money for us."

Other parents find that some generally helpful approaches do not nevertheless lead to improvement with their children. "One approach that never worked was Hooked on Phonics," says Linda in Southern California. "That was when I began to realize how my son learns. He viewed things from the front to the back. For example, when reading, if the end of the word was provided, then you added in the first sound to make a word. He couldn't figure it out. But if it was reversed, like Abeka presents phonics, he could get it."

> Unlicensed and even licensed professionals may prey on desperate families seeking to ease their children's learning and health difficulties.

One generally accepted method of working with special needs children is providing a huge amount of structure to their environments. The prevailing notion is that children who study in a controlled setting with a specific timeframe and work assignments will stay focused, thus allowing them to learn. In school settings this has certainly achieved some success in controlling behaviors, but this practice does not allow the child to develop the abilities to work independently or to broaden skills in areas of interest.

Jill, the Louisiana homeschool parent of a thirteen-year-old son with brain trauma, shuns the structured approach. "Typical self-paced, one-set-way programs don't work for my son," she says. "He needs flexibility. He has no short-term memory, so trying to drill information is not useful—memorization doesn't work for him. Showing my son how to find the information is the best way to reach him."

Rhonda in Michigan agrees: "Anytime we attempt anything remotely similar to traditional schooling, we fail. My son needs lots of movement, music, lots of breaks, and the ability to say 'I need to do this later.' Even though traditional sit-down schooling might be useful for some, it doesn't work for everyone."

DIAGNOSIS BY SCHOOL OFFICIALS

CHILDREN ENROLLED IN school typically receive their first and sometimes only diagnosis from a teacher or other educational support staff. Although credentialed school personnel may seem qualified to determine a child's learning difficulties, many have little to no formal training in psychology or any field outside of education. The exceptions are those school counselors who have cross-trained as family therapists and who possess proper training in assessment and intervention. The background of most school psychologists, however, is that of a psychometrist—one who is knowledgeable in administering and interpreting standardized assessments, not necessarily in other aspects of psychology.

"The school psychologist had given my daughter an intensive psychological evaluation," recalls Linda in Northern California. "But he didn't have a clue to her diagnosis. So they sent her to a school for the severely emotionally disturbed (SED) for two years." It was later determined that Linda's daughter has Asperger's Syndrome.

In addition to evaluating children's level of education, many teachers, principals, counselors, and school psychologists have told parents to medicate their children with psychotropic drugs. This practice has been coming under fire, and in the summer of 2001 the Connecticut General Assembly unanimously voted to prohibit school officials from recommending psychiatric drugs for children. The measure, which is the first law of its kind, only allows school officials to recommend that parents seek medical evaluations for their children. The first mention of medication must come from a physician; educators and allied school staff cannot offer opinions as medical or psychological diagnoses.

This is exactly the approach that Dawn in Wisconsin followed years ago with her now eighteen-year-old son. Yet taking what appeared to be the right path at the time didn't deliver her family to an optimum destination. Acting on a recommendation of the school psychologist, Dawn and her husband took their son to a large hospital facility for two days of testing to determine what was behind his learning difficulties. The testing yielded a diagnosis of ADD, for which the family pediatrician prescribed psychostimulant medication. During the next four years, a variety of medications were used in attempts to control their son's ADD. At one time, Dawn had forgotten to refill her son's medication, which resulted in his not taking the morning dosage. After a week without morning medication, she received a call from the school requesting a meeting. She recalls, "The teachers and principal all told us about their concerns for our son. They felt something had changed in the previous week. They claimed that he 'woke up' during the morning hours but was withdrawn in the afternoon. When I told them that he wasn't taking his medication in the morning, they were very angry and told me that he needed the medication."

> Although credentialed school personnel may seem qualified to determine a child's learning difficulties, many have little to no formal training in psychology.

At that point, Dawn realized the medication was doing more harm than good and advised the school officials that her son would not resume taking the medication. She pointed out that, after all, the teachers were the ones to notice that her son was more awake without the drugs. The family's decision didn't sit well with the school staff. The additional announcement that they were considering homeschooling was received with a pronouncement that this would be the worst thing that Dawn and her husband could possibly do for their son.

THERAPY TIP

Over the years, I have found that some therapists are supportive and others are not. When calling therapists, you need to find one who is willing to work with you. Explain that you want a "home program" developed and that you'd like to be able to sit in on sessions and repeat the same process at home. This is the best way to make outside services truly work for you.

—BERYL, MICHIGAN PARENT OF A TEN-YEAR-OLD HIGH-FUNCTIONING AUTISTIC SON

Dawn's son has been homeschooled for the past five years and is preparing to graduate this semester. The family later learned that the initial ADD diagnosis was incorrect. Another psychologist recognized his traits and behaviors as related to Asperger's Syndrome.

NIGHTMARES ON THE THERAPY-GO-ROUND

PUBLIC SCHOOLS AND their methods aren't the sole targets for parental scorn or anguish. Medical and mental professionals rank high on the complaint scale. "I've had a long and terrible experience with the traditional methods and treatment for ADHD," laments Victoria, a Louisiana parent of a thirteen-year-old son. "I think this is one group of children horribly abused by the drug companies and HMOs that have a stronghold over treatment. It doesn't help that the psychiatric community generally views homeschooling as 'giving up' on your child."

Tracy in California recalls the numerous roadblocks she encountered when she first started to seek assistance for her daughter's reading difficulties. "Lots of specialists wanted to test my daughter's IQ, while others suggested mental health therapy. The bottom line," she states, "was that she and I both knew she was intelligent. We didn't need to spend a lot of money and time on tests to figure that out. We just wanted her to be able to communicate that intelligence without the frustration."

Seeking second and even third opinions from professionals is a wise move, but it does set the stage to completely overwhelm parents and children. Many parents are aghast to discover how a variety of mental health professionals can render a variety of diagnoses for the same child. Parents may start to wonder if all the diagnoses are correct, meaning that their child is severely disturbed. California homeschooling parent Tamara remembers all too well how her son was on-track to receive a "collection" of professionally issued diagnoses. "One family therapist who saw him twice said after the first meeting, 'There's nothing wrong with him.' After the second, she said, 'He's definitely ADHD.' She also felt he was depressed." Tamara, however, wasn't completely confident in that assessment of her son and sought consults with other professionals. After numerous psychologists, psychiatrists, and family therapists weighed in their assessments, her son had amassed quite an array of diagnoses, including ADHD and oppositional defiant disorder. Furthermore, Tamara was frequently blamed for a variety of transgressions, from possessing weak parenting skills to causing immaturity in her son because they homeschooled. She was advised to set more stringent limits on her son, to use more time-out sessions, and to make him do standards (repetitive line writing). Other parents who were familiar with her son also "offered" a variety of opinions, ranging from "psychopath" to "gifted, albeit spirited." However, one homeschooling mother with an ADD daughter steered Tamara toward a perceptual motor (PM) specialist, who diagnosed several deficiencies.

This specialist felt that Tamara's son possessed a lateral input deficiency, which affects reading and writing, and no separation of sensory input. It was ascertained that the boy had never developed his abdominal muscles and was compensating by using his back muscles, straining them to overfatigue. "*That, not ADHD,*" cites Tamara, "was the reason he couldn't sit still for long. It's quite likely he has no ADHD at all."

> Many parents are aghast to discover how a variety of mental health professionals can render a variety of diagnoses for the same child.

Further assessment by an occupational therapist added more missing pieces to the puzzle. Tamara's son had balance problems originating in his ear and difficulty with small motor skills. After focusing on these sensory integration issues, rather than the proposed psychological ones, Tamara's son is making progress.

Keep in mind that each psychologist or therapist possesses an individual perspective regarding what causes difficulties in emotional and behavioral functioning. These professionals are providing you with opinions based on their individual training, experience, and bias. Also realize that it's extremely difficult to assess a child over a short period of time and in surroundings unfamiliar to him or her. Your child may act completely different (for better or worse) away from home when fielding seemingly odd questions from a complete stranger.

In these cases, it's best to follow your intuition and the comfort level of your child. If you sense that your child is uncomfortable with a professional, don't use that person, even if he's highly acclaimed in his field.

HOW-TO'S OF LOCATING THERAPY

FINDING A THERAPIST who is both skilled and supportive of homeschooling is a find indeed! Now, you ask, how do I go about locating professionals who will meet the needs of my family? Patience, perseverance, and asking the right questions are key.

Education and Training

What is the therapist's education and training? It doesn't matter so much that she holds sterling credentials from an Ivy League school, but it does matter that she has been to school, is licensed (or is in the process), and has had a variety of experiences (many during graduate school). Also important is how often she participates in and what types of studies she pursues in her own continuing education. If she only attends the minimum required to maintain her license or if she seems to attend seminars in exotic places, she's probably more interested in making money than bettering herself, her professional expertise, and the individuals she treats. You don't want to work with a person whose sole purpose for entering a profession is based on goals toward abundant wealth and tax write-offs.

Specialists Aren't Necessarily Better

What experience with your child's specific condition does the therapist have? If you suspect that your child has ADD, and a prospective therapist has minimal experience with this disorder, don't necessarily rule him out. The ADD specialist will undoubtedly proclaim your child ADD, too. Therapists with a general background could bring a fresh approach to understanding your child's difficulties.

Homeschool Friendly

How does the prospective therapist feel about homeschooling? Don't think that you need to use your child's successes to convince a therapist who is not accepting of homeschooling. If the therapist is adamantly opposed to home education, chances are that your child's care will suffer. It also isn't necessary to find a therapist who whole-heartedly embraces homeschooling. The main concern is locating one who is open-minded and receptive to your child.

> If a therapist is adamantly opposed to home education, chances are that your child's care will suffer.

Nuts and Bolts

What is the financial cost of each session, and does your insurance cover this particular type of therapy? If so, for how long? You'll also want to know how often your child will need to see the therapist, the duration of each session, and the long-term time commitment. Ask questions such as, How does the therapist handle emergencies? Is the therapist available outside office hours, or does the therapist refer emergencies to a colleague?

OTHER MEDICAL PROFESSIONALS

USE THE FOLLOWING information not only for those practitioners providing services, but also in choosing those whom your child may need to see on a regular basis, especially the dentist!

Your Child's Dentist

Many dentists, especially pediatric specialists, insist upon seeing children alone, without the parents. The rationale behind this practice is that children will behave more appropriately without the parent in the room. Going to the dentist can be a frightening experience for children and adults. Differently abled children are especially vulnerable, as many of them tend to be fearful of strange situations, are intolerant of shrill sounds, and have difficulty processing verbal directions.

Some dentists who work with difficult children may opt to sedate them with medication. When we took our son for his first dental appointment at the age of three, the trauma he suffered could've had a lifelong negative impact on his ability to trust dentists. We were not told of the "child only" policy when we made our son's appointment or upon checking in. It wasn't until our son was called in and my husband attempted to accompany him that we were informed our son would be just fine alone. Of course, he wasn't. He was upset at being separated from his father and taken into a strange room with unknown people. Our son's cries quickly escalated into screams while he tried to leave to find his dad. After an upsetting few minutes (which seemed like hours), my son was released. My husband was advised that future appointments would require special scheduling so that the staff could place our son in restraints and administer psychostimulant drugs. We vowed to locate another dentist whose bedside manner would take into account our child's needs. Phoning a variety of highly recommended dentists in our area yielded somber results—nearly all of them believed in seeing children alone and sedating them if necessary.

We tried a few dentists who reluctantly allowed us to accompany our son. But after his first experience, he would panic at the mention of "going to the dentist." One of my husband's childhood friends heard of our son's dental encounters and referred us to her dentist, who has been a lifesaver. He's a family-oriented practitioner who has shown compassion and understanding toward children's individual differences. He quickly gained my son's confidence.

Developmental Optometry

The following was originally published in the *California Homeschooler* (September/October 1996). It is reprinted here with permission from Lillian Jones and the Homeschool Association of California (P.O. Box 868, Davis, CA 95617, 888-HSC-4440, www.hsc.org).

"Mom! Look! Can we get these?" My twelve-year-old son eagerly held out a trilogy of thick adult sci-fi books he had just found in the used bookstore. Stunned, I warily paged through one, wondering how we could find time for them. We already had a shelf of good books lined up at home for me to read aloud to him. "But I'll read these myself!" he protested. A standoff. Since they were only a dollar apiece, I gave in, although I was puzzled. I had not yet made the connection with his sessions in vision skill training.

Ethan had good reading skills but had never read books just for pleasure and certainly never a thick one with fine print. Something was changing dramatically. He started voraciously into the first of those three books on the way home, and had them all read within the week. Then he started picking up books around the house and devouring those. He noticed how curiously large the print seemed in the fourth and fifth grade level books he had read before. "Boy, these books don't have much in them," he observed.

It was then that I realized a small miracle was in progress. Ethan had recently completed over two dozen hours of vision therapy with a developmental optometrist, and the results of his work were now materializing.

During the initial screening test, the doctor had found that Ethan had excellent reading skills, but had to work very hard to process information as his eyes tracked across the page. Current research indicates that approximately one of every four children has learning related vision skill problems. The National Society for the Prevention of Blindness estimates that 10 million children in the United States have undiagnosed vision problems. Research also shows that seven out of ten juvenile delinquents have undiagnosed vision problems.

Teachers, and even parents, often label kids as lazy, unmotivated, looking for attention, or learning disabled when, in fact, undetected vision problems are frequently at the root of their difficulties. Children who seem to struggle with learning that involves the visual process (reading, writing, math, etc.) need to have comprehensive, learning-related vision exams.

"20/20 vision is not enough," says Bev Ehlers of Parents Active for Vision Education (PAVE), a national nonprofit organization founded by parents and teachers of children who suffered the effects of undiagnosed vision problems. "It doesn't relate to the way we read, type, write, or do math," she explains, "and yet it's the way most of us have our vision tested."

PAVE's free information packet explains that a child with 20/20 eyesight may still have problems with eye movement control, eye teaming ability, sustaining clear focus at near and far, sharpness of sight at the reading distance, eye-hand coordination and visual perception, and memory. A good learning-related vision test should evaluate twenty such subskills of vision.

Parents are urged to have their children evaluated before they are introduced to reading. Margie Thompson, PAVE founder and president, says, "A child who is experiencing a learning or behavior problem should have a developmental vision exam. An undiagnosed or uncorrected vision problem will hamper a child for the rest of his or her life. Learning is joyful for the child with strong visual, auditory, motor and thinking skills. These are all learned skills. We create failure for children when we focus on what they learn before how they learn."

An article (included in PAVE's packet) in the May/June 1992 issue of *Natural Health* tells the story of one family's twin sons, for whom two ophthalmologists recommended surgery to correct "turned-out" eye problems. The doctors both insisted that visual training is "nonsense" and "voodoo," but the family held out for vision training with a developmental optometrist. The children's mother recounted: "I told my sons that I was writing a magazine article about their 'eye work' and asked them if they had anything they'd like to say. 'Maybe when other people find out what happened to us it will help them too,' said one son. 'And maybe some kids won't have to have surgery,' added the other twin. 'It worked for us, 'cause now we can really see.'"

Ophthalmologists (medical doctors who specialize in diseases of the eye) are often unaware, and sometimes skeptical, of the benefits of developmental optometry. Optometrists and ophthalmologists have entirely different training, and optometrists will send patients to ophthalmologists for certain conditions, since not all vision problems can be corrected by vision training. A developmental optometrist puts the patient through procedures that result in retraining the brain to take in visual information—the child's internal computer is reprogrammed with new vision skills.

It is important to determine that a practitioner of vision therapy is a certified developmental optometrist, sometimes known as a behavioral optometrist. To be certified as a fellow of the College of Optometrists in Vision Development (COVD), an optometrist practices vision therapy for three years and completes oral and written testing and case reports. An optometrist may also do effective vision therapy as a member or an associate of the COVD.

Last night when I popped in to say goodnight to my son, he was curled up in bed with a book and had two more piled next to him. "Can I just finish this chapter?" he pleaded. This vision therapy has created a whole new problem in our lives: How do we get this kid to sleep when there are so many good books to be read?

I can't reiterate enough that your role as parent provides you with the unparalleled ability to serve as your child's expert and key advocate. It may seem that many medical and mental health professionals possess the opinion that parents should take a back seat when it comes to assisting in their children's assessment and treatment. But there are many professionals who actually do consider parents to be part of their children's team of practitioners. While it might take time and energy to locate these gems, don't settle for anything less for your child!

SIMPLE STARTING POINTS

✦ *Ask family and friends for referrals.* Those who are supportive of your homeschooling may know medical and mental health professionals.

✦ *Don't limit yourself to specialists.* Family practice physicians possess a wealth of knowledge and experience. Many of your child's special needs can be addressed by family practitioners. When they can't help, they can serve as a case manager, providing referrals and tracking progress.

✦ *Regularly observe and assess your child's progress.* Remember that children are constantly growing and changing. Keep a journal of progress (and regressions) to share with practitioners during consultation sessions.

RESOURCES

Dietary Interventions

Books

Bell, Rachel, Howard Peiper, Nina Anderson, and Doris Rapp. *The A.D.D. and A.D.H.D. Diet! Updated: A Comprehensive Look at Contributing Factors and Natural Treatments for Symptoms of Attention Deficit Disorder and Hyperactivity.* Safe Goods, 2001.

Feingold, Ben F. *Why Your Child Is Hyperactive.* Random House, 1985.

Lewis, Lisa. *Special Diets for Special Kids.* Future Horizons, 1998.

Rapp, Doris. *Is This Your Child? Discovering and Treating Unrecognized Allergies in Children and Adults.* William Morrow, 1991.

Catalogs

Safe Goods, 561 Shunpike Road, Sheffield, MA 01257, 888-628-8731, www.safegoodspub.com

Web Sites

Tammy Glaser's Web Site: home.earthlink.net/%7Etammyglaser798 /pamela.html

Dyslexia and Reading

Books

Davis, Ronald G., with Eldon M. Braun. *The Gift of Dyslexia: Why Some of the Smartest People Can't Read and How They Can Learn.* Perigee, 1997.

Oelwein, Patricia Logan. *Teaching Reading to Children with Down Syndrome: A Guide for Parents and Teachers.* Woodbine House, 1995.

Organizations

AVKO Dyslexia Research Foundation, 3084 W. Willard Road, Suite W, Clio, MI 48420-7801, 810-686-9283, www.avko.org

Davis Dyslexia Association International, 1601 Bayshore Highway, Suite 245, Burlingame, CA 94010, 650-692-7141, www.dyslexia.com

General Special Needs

Books

Greenspan, Stanley. *The Child with Special Needs: Encouraging Intellectual and Emotional Growth.* Perseus Press, 1998.

Catalogs

Edmark Corporation, Attention: Special Needs, P.O. Box 97021, Redmond, WA 98073-9721; 800-691-2986; www.edmark.com/

Flaghouse, 601 Flaghouse Drive, Hasbrouck Heights, NJ 07604-3116, 800-793-7900, www.flaghouse.com

Pro-Ed, 8700 Shoal Creek Boulevard, Austin, TX 78757, 800-897-3202, www.proedinc.com/store/index.php

Super Duper Publications, P.O. Box 24997, Greenville, SC 29616, 800-277-8737, www.superduperinc.com

Organizations

The Council for Exceptional Children, 1110 North Glebe Road, Suite 300, Arlington, VA 22201-5704, 888-CEC-SPED, www.cec.sped.org/

Learning Disabilities Association of America, 4156 Library Road, Pittsburgh, PA 15234-1349, 412-341-1515, www.LDAAmerica.org/

National Institute of Mental Health (NIMH), 6001 Executive Boulevard, Room 8184, MSC 9663, Bethesda, MD 20892-9663, 301-443-4513, www.nimh.nih.gov

Web Sites

Educational Resources Information Center (ERIC), Clearinghouse on Disabilities and Gifted Education: www.ericec.org/faqs.html

Homeschool Friendly Medical and Mental Health Professionals: www.bayshoreeducational.com/specialdocs.html

LDOnline: www.ldonline.org/

Professional Organizations

American Association for Marriage and Family Therapy (AAMFT), 1133 15th Street NW, Suite 300, Washington, DC 20005-2710, 202-452-0109, www.aamft.org

American Occupational Therapy Association (AOTA), P.O. Box 31220, Bethesda, MD 20824-1220, 301-652-2682, www.aota.org

American Psychological Association (APA), 750 First Street NE, Washington, DC 20002-4242, 800-374-2721, www.apa.org

National Association of Social Workers, 750 First Street NE, Suite 700, Washington, DC 20002-4241, 800-638-8799, www.naswdc.org

Sensory Integration/Occupational Therapy

Books

Ayres, A. Jean. *Sensory Integration and the Child.* Western Psychological Services, 1979.

Kranowitz, Carol Stock. *The Out-of-Sync Child: Recognizing and Coping with Sensory Integration Dysfunction.* Perigree, 1998.

Catalogs

OT Ideas, 124 Morris Turnpike, Randolph, NJ 07869, 877-768-4332, www.otideas.com

Shoebox Tasks, 272 Old Weaverville Road, Asheville, NC 28804, 828-645-9615, www.shoeboxtasks.com

SouthpawEnterprises, P.O. Box 1047, Dayton, OH 45401, 800-228-1698, www.southpawenterprises.com

Sport Time Abilitations, One Sportime Way, Atlanta, GA 30340
800-444-5700 or 770-449-5700, www.abilitations.com

Methods

Brain Gym Edu-Kinesthetics, P.O. Box 3395, Ventura, CA 93006-
3395, 888-388-9898, www.braingym.com

Organizations

Educational Kinesiology Foundation, 1575 Spinnaker Drive, Suite
204B, Ventura, CA 93001, 800-356-2109, www.braingrym.org
Sensory Integration International, 1514 Cabrillo Avenue, Torrance,
CA 90501, 310-320-2335, www.sensoryint.com/

Social Skills Training

Books

Forman, Susan. *Coping Skills Interventions for Children and Adoles-
cents.* Jossey-Bass, 1993.
Gray, Carol. *Comic Strip Conversations.* Future Horizons, 1994.
Gray, Carol. *The New Social Stories: Illustrated Edition.* Future Hori-
zons, 2000.
Marshall, Duke, Stephen Nowicki Jr., and Elisabeth Martin. *Teach-
ing Your Child the Language of Social Success.* Peachtree, 1996.
Nowicki, Stephen Jr., and Duke Marshall. *Helping the Child Who
Doesn't Fit In: Clinical Psychologists Decipher the Hidden Dimen-
sions of Social Rejection.* Peachtree, 1992.

Catalogs

Creative Therapy Associates (feelings poster), 7709 Hamilton Avenue,
Cincinnati, OH 45231-3103, 800-448-9145, www.ctherapy.com
Future Horizons, 721 W. Abram Street, Arlington, TX 76013, 800-
489-0727, www.futurehorizons-autism.com/
Peachtree Publications, 1700 Chattahoochee Avenue, Atlanta, GA
30318-2112, 800-241-0113, www.peachtree-online.com

Web Sites

The Gray Center for Social Learning and Understanding: The Gray Center (social story guidelines), P.O. Box 67, Jenison, MI 49429, 616-667-2396, www.thegraycenter.org/social.htm

Therapeutic Resources: Communicative Disorders

Books

Lapish, Marisa. *Straight Talk*, Volumes 1 and 2. Available through Nathhan, P.O. Box 39, Porthill, ID 83853, www.nathhan.com.

Raz, Mirla G. *Help Me Talk Right: How to Correct a Child's Lisp in 15 Easy Lessons*. Gerstenweitz, 1993.

Raz, Mirla G. *Help Me Talk Right: How to Teach a Child to Say the "L" Sound in 15 Easy Lessons*. Gerstenweitz, 1999.

Raz, Mirla G. *Help Me Talk Right: How to Teach a Child to Say the "R" Sound in 15 Easy Lessons*. Gerstenweitz, 1996.

Methods

Earobics, 990 Grove Street, Evanston, IL 60201, 888-328-8199, www.earobics.com

FastForward, Scientific Learning, 300 Frank H. Ogawa Plaza, Suite 500, Oakland, CA 94612, 888-665-9707, www.scilearn.com/

Lindamood-Bell Learning Processes, 416 Higuera Street, San Luis Obispo, CA 93401, 800-233-1819, www.lblp.com

LinguiSystems, 3100 4th Avenue, East Moline, IL 61244, 800-776-4332, www.linguisystems.com

Organizations

John Tracy Clinic (deaf resources), 806 West Adams Boulevard, Los Angeles, CA 90007, 213-748-5481, www.jtc.org

Web Sites

Carol's Speech and Language Disorders Professional Resources: www.angelfire.com/nj/speechlanguage/SLResources.html

Vision

Organizations

Parents Active for Vision Education (PAVE), 4135 54th Place, San Diego, CA 92105-2303, 800-PAVE-988, www.pave-eye.com /~vision/

Web Sites

The Vision Connection: www.kidscite.net

Web Sites

Be an Informed Consumer, by Leslie E. Packer, Ph.D.: www .tourettesyndrome.net/informed_consumer.htm

12

FINAL ENCOURAGEMENTS

In This Chapter

+ You are your child's best expert
+ Identify and use support
+ Do your homework
+ Prepare for life changes
+ Work toward a good fit between child and parent
+ Resist the urge to compare
+ Welcome flexibility into your life
+ Give homeschooling some time
+ Enjoy the benefits
+ This is your family's decision

© Photodisc

*T*HIS BOOK HAS taken you on a journey through the various joys and challenges that homeschoolers face with their differently abled children. Many parents have opened their hearts and minds to provide you with a glimpse into what you might face should you choose to follow this path.

Many of these parents wanted to share a few final thoughts. In this chapter, some parents discuss how their own children have blossomed to show you how yours, too, can experience successes. Others proffer cautionary notes to provide you with the reality check that although homeschooling is beneficial, it won't completely solve your problems. As with most major life changes, prepare wisely for potential challenges and should the obstacles not materialize, the fruits reaped are yours to savor.

YOU ARE YOUR CHILD'S BEST EXPERT

SINCE YOUR CHILD's birth, you have always been his first teacher. Depending on your child's development, you were the one who encouraged your child to smile, point, wave, sit, walk, and talk. In many cases, schools have attempted to extract parents from their primary roles as soon as children reach the age of compulsory attendance. Parents are told to step aside so that the specialists can control the children for the next twelve or more years. Yet, you're the one who knows the most about your child's educational, medical, social, and emotional needs. You are the expert who deals with the daily issues that arise with your differently abled child. If you're a parent who has relinquished your teaching duties, here's your opportunity to regain them.

"Learn all that you can about your child's special needs," says Susan, a Louisiana homeschooling parent. "Let your child pursue areas that interest him or her. Go with your instincts no matter what school officials say—no one knows your child better than you do!"

Marita, a homeschooling mother to an eleven-year-old Asperger's Syndrome son in Australia, agrees wholeheartedly. She feels it's crucial to read and learn as much as possible about your child's special needs. "Concentrate on areas in which your child really needs the most help." She adds, "It will not necessarily be academics."

IDENTIFY AND USE SUPPORT

RESEARCHING AND LOCATING more in-depth supports are a necessity, especially in the early days. Examine your current support system and ask yourself whether these friends, family, and professionals are going to be there for you as you journey into homeschooling. Tamara maintains, "Some homeschoolers, especially unschoolers, feel that it's cheating to get help from experts and use tutors and specialists. They try to do it all themselves, because that's 'homeschooling.' But it's not. It's about giving the child the best education possible, not about furthering the homeschooling movement." She concludes, "In other words, we don't have to be super-mom or super-dad and do it all ourselves. We can and should use other people who can help."

It's obviously not necessary to draw a homeschool-only circle of confidantes around yourself, but it's extremely helpful to have at least one home educator to whom you can connect. If you don't know other homeschoolers in your community, join an e-mail list for support. Elaine in Texas urges, "Join a support group or an e-mail support list and find out what everyone else is doing, then you can get ideas and also know it's been done before."

Remember to take care of yourself! You need to keep some vestige of your pre-homeschooling life; otherwise, resentment toward your children and others in your life may grow. If you've left a career you love to homeschool full time, stay abreast in your field and connect with colleagues regularly. Those who've left a less than satisfying job can take time to learn new skills that can prepare for future employment. Many homeschooling parents report the gratification of

SMALL MIRACLES

Since coming home, my mostly nonverbal child learned to say "happy." It is the only word in her limited vocabulary that doesn't get her something she needs. Rather, it conveys something that brings her pleasure.

—LISA IN MICHIGAN, PARENT TO A FIFTEEN-YEAR-OLD AUTISTIC DAUGHTER learning alongside their children, whether for a new livelihood or for other pursuits purely for personal satisfaction. Regardless of what you were doing prior to homeschooling, take time to daydream about future possibilities while caring for some of your personal needs. Linda in Southern California offers, "As enjoyable as being with the children is, it's also important to take care of yourself. Have a secondary source (who loves your children) to help you with the kids or to do things to help yourself. For example, my husband takes the kids evenings so I can usually do extra study for classes."

DO YOUR HOMEWORK

YOU'RE PROBABLY THINKING that there is so much to do before even beginning to homeschool your children! Some parents stress the importance of first organizing your home and lifestyle. Then again, many of us never manage to accomplish this within a lifetime, and yet we still find a way to homeschool. The main prerequisites are making the decision, knowing your legal rights, and having the desire to nurture your child's education.

"Educate yourself," advises Lisa in Michigan. "Talk to people who've had a variety of experiences. Keep some brief notes on your own homeschooling and read them periodically to remember how far you've come when you feel you're getting nowhere." She further advises the new homeschooler to "know your rights and assume your responsibilities with joy. This experience has made me realize how precious freedom is."

LJ in Oregon strongly believes in including children in the decision to homeschool. She also suggests that you allow ample time to deschool both your child and yourself. If your child wants to try homeschooling, allow her the freedom to enjoy her interests while you take time to research the vast expanses afforded by homeschooling. LJ adds, "Get to know the *real* child rather than the one the school presented to you, and only do activities that are fun for both you and your child."

Linda in Southern California advocates preparing back-up plans in the event of unforeseen problems, particularly in the therapeutic realm. "Have it clear in your mind how to handle the various needs that may arise with your child. Know where to get the help your kid

LEARNING WITHOUT A DESK

Homeschooling is better than public school because I can go at my own pace. I don't get picked on by the other kids. It's easier and more interesting. I can lie on my bed, the floor, outside, or wherever I want to study. I don't *have* to sit at a desk. When I was in public school, sitting at a desk drove me crazy. If I moved, I thought I would get yelled at by the teacher. So all I could think was, sit still, sit still, sit still, and I couldn't pay attention to what the teacher was saying or doing.

I like homeschooling because I can study things that I find interesting. Not everything is interesting to me, but we can find ways to make it more fun and seem to come alive. I had to catch up on lots of things, so I haven't had a lot of time to do all that I would like. I started homeschool in the seventh grade, five weeks before school ended. Yet, I only knew stuff through the second grade.

I'm now in my senior year and am only one-half credit short of graduating according to the public school guidelines. So I feel I have come a very long way in a very short time. I never would have been able to do catch up had I stayed in public school.

—JOSH HURNING IN WISCONSIN, EIGHTEEN YEARS OLD. DIAGNOSED WITH ASPERGER'S SYNDROME, JOSH HAS HOMESCHOOLED FOR FIVE YEARS AND PLANS TO PURSUE AN APPRENTICESHIP PROGRAM IN EITHER WELDING OR HEAVY MACHINERY OPERATIONS. A COMPUTER WHIZ AND BOOKWORM, HE IS ALSO AN ESTEEMED ALUMNUS OF THE CALVIN AND HOBBES CURRICULUM.

may need. When we first started, I had doctors and other specialists lined up in case I needed more assistance."

PREPARE FOR LIFE CHANGES

YOU'VE UNDOUBTEDLY MADE at least a few major changes in your life—becoming a parent, partnering with a loved one, choosing a career, or pursuing higher education. All major decisions have affected your life with an assortment of both positives and negatives. Making the decision to homeschool your children is no different. Examine your present lifestyle and determine whether you're willing to give up some aspects of it to make room for others.

Understand the Responsibilities

Louisiana homeschooling parent Victoria has witnessed the consequences of those families who approached homeschooling with less than a firm commitment to lifestyle change. "I personally feel that this is a better approach to education. However, I've come across many families who 'drop out' of homeschooling. I advise parents to be aware of the costs and the time involved; it will be difficult if you're a dentist and your wife is a full-time real estate agent. You cannot expect the housekeeper or child caregiver to take up this responsibility."

Understand Yourself

Parents frequently realize that the changes that take place when transitioning to homeschooling are more internal and personal. Parents start to recall aspects of their own childhoods and may start to notice a number of shared traits, positive and negative, with their children that were never before realized. Some may blame themselves for passing along "faulty genes." Others, however, refuse to accept the similarities, expecting the child to change so the parent doesn't have to experience emotional pain. Remember that accepting your own differences is an opportunity for healing and personal growth.

Julia, a New York homeschooling parent to a twelve-year-old high-functioning autistic son, advises, "The change will begin with you, first in your heart and then in your actions. Like a spider web, everything will interconnect. I've seen incredible changes in families after autistic spectrum kids come home."

Understand Your Child

As you homeschool, you will start to realize your child's potential. Some parents may have never viewed their children as anything other than a "handicapped child." This was most likely an unconscious thought. But as parents homeschool, they often realize that they have never fully grasped and appreciated their children's talents. "It's wonderful to see parents soften," adds Julia. "They let go of the blame, and the love comes tumbling out."

WORK TOWARD A GOOD FIT BETWEEN CHILD AND PARENT

MANY PARENTS RELISH the notion of spending time together with their children and sharing, or at least observing, their accomplishments, joys, and even struggles. To others, the notion of having a child around all day is nothing less than a curse. Even before my family started homeschooling, I was amazed at how many parents told me they couldn't wait until their children reached school-age so the parents wouldn't have to deal with the children so much. I'd often come away from those discussions wondering why these individuals brought children into the world.

On the other hand, even parents who dearly love and want the best for their children may find their personalities colliding with their children. You may find yourself faced with the prospect of having to homeschool a child with whom you share a fractious relationship. You may wonder if such a task is feasible. Attempting to work through personality clashes or differences of opinion while homeschooling can be an effort in futility, producing results in neither area. However, taking the time to work through the difficult aspects of the parent-child relationship can bear a lifetime of benefits. Work with a family therapist, psychologist, or clergy member trained in relationships. Homeschooling and being with your child during the day allows you to incorporate relationship building with academics. Ann, a Pennsylvania homeschooler of three, adds, "Make it a matter of sincere prayer."

Ann also warns of a different kind of challenge: "Mothers, think very seriously about homeschooling male teenagers. Young men sometimes find it demeaning to take direction from their mothers after a certain age—once the hormones start to flow." She advises, "Any mother starting to homeschool a young man in puberty needs to seriously think about the impact of hormones. Sons may suddenly notice that Mom is not as tall as she used to be; not quite as smart as he used to think; and that it isn't too cool having to account to your mother, not only for your whereabouts, but also your schoolwork. Periodically I'd remind 'The Big Guy' that he could return to public high school any time."

While Ann's experience was with a male adolescent, parents of both genders may find themselves faced with emotional scenes they might not have experienced if their children had been in school all day. Then again, many homeschooling parents report being able to re-establish a long lost relationship with their teen child.

RESIST THE URGE TO COMPARE

PARENTS OF DIFFERENTLY abled children tend to view other same-age counterparts with a comparing eye. This is a natural occurrence in that mentally many of us play "what if?" We wonder what our children would be like if they could succeed in the ways we imagine those other, seemingly "normal" children succeed. Your child—differences, difficulties, and all—is an individual with a unique collection of insights and strengths. In school, we learn to compare our social and academic weaknesses against the strengths of others. This practice can be discarded when you remove your child from school.

"Don't compare your special needs child to peers or siblings," insists Kerri in South Dakota. "Don't look at where he is academically, look at how far he has come. Just look at the big picture and ask yourself, What is best for him?" She continues, "Time, nurturing, and encouragement from a parent will do more for a child than getting frustrated in a classroom where he can't individualize his unique learning styles and needs."

WELCOME FLEXIBILITY INTO YOUR LIFE

IF YOU'RE THINKING that flexibility is not a word synonymous with your life, welcome to the world of homeschooling! Not only have you added a new word to your personal vocabulary list, but you're also about to experience a whole new lifestyle—one that often thrives on uncertainty.

Linda in Southern California encourages families to focus on the positive aspects of flexibility, such as not having a set schedule. She marvels at the days when her family accomplishes much, yet they work effortlessly and with pleasure—unlike those days when her sons were enrolled in school and nothing more than stress was achieved. "Be flexible!" she asserts. "You need to be adaptable, because the best plan covering the various areas of need or educational exposures may look great on paper, but in practicality, it almost always gets adapted."

That flexibility also requires altering your thoughts on what activities count as educational. Texas homeschooling parent Elaine cautions, "Don't expect every day to be perfect or that 'education' must only take place at certain times. Some of our best days have been when my eight-year-old son and I worked on a K'Nex structure (a great fine motor activity) or when we've had a read-a-thon day."

There are also times when you're committed to homeschooling but something isn't quite right. It might be that a long-term family problem has arisen or that your child, for whatever reasons, needs a different setting. Through the years, Jill, a foster parent in California, has cared for more than forty special needs children, many of whom she's homeschooled. She stresses that parents need to follow their hearts and intuition when determining whether their children's needs can be met through homeschooling. She cautions, however, "Keep in mind that needs can change. Stay flexible and be willing to drop the homeschooling if it no longer meets the needs of your child, your family, or yourself."

This does occur to some families. Should it happen to you and your family, don't shoulder the burden of blame upon yourself. Blame is not a necessary component of change. Acceptance is, as is keeping one eye focused toward the future. One of the beauties of homeschooling is that you can always go back to it.

GIVE HOMESCHOOLING SOME TIME

IMPATIENCE AND HOMESCHOOLING don't mix. A common notion among parents is to remove a child from school and home-school for a brief period in an attempt to fill academic gaps. While this is certainly an option, you need to understand that a few months of a one-on-one nurturing learning environment cannot overturn years of substandard mass education. If your child does get up-to-speed by the school's standards, chances are he'll regress (academically, emotionally, or both) upon returning to school. Take your time and re-evaluate your needs and goals periodically.

Lisa, the Michigan parent of two children, one of whom is a high-functioning autistic daughter, advises, "Use the summer to experiment—just work with your child a few hours a week. If you are pulling your child out of school, don't give up homeschooling too quickly. The first few weeks and months are a real test for both parent and child. Give it at least a one-year trial. You can always go back to the old way."

Many families follow an afterschooling approach before completely committing to no school. "Afterschooling" is the term used by many people who send their children to school, yet work intensely with them after school. Parents often realize that if they eliminate the school to work at home with their children, the pace is less frenetic. No longer is there a need to rush through the afterschool hours to reteach a child what he didn't learn during the school day.

Before deciding to homeschool, Rhonda in Michigan found positives and negatives in educating her son after school. "If I hadn't afterschooled Cole from kindergarten to fourth grade, he wouldn't have learned anything! I retaught the entire day, and we covered all that the teacher had done each day. When he had a cooperative teacher, this was easy; when he didn't, I had to do a lot of guessing. We always had an extra set of textbooks at home, which helped a lot." However, she cautions, "I now regret doing this because I fear I may have contributed to my son's stress. He was angry and violent because his day at school was extremely difficult most of the time."

SMALL MIRACLES

There's nothing greater than being involved with your child on a daily basis and watching him "get it." When the light comes on in a certain subject and his face brightens, it makes any struggles you have endured, all worthwhile.

—DAWN IN WISCONSIN, PARENT TO AN EIGHTEEN-YEAR-OLD ASPERGER'S SYNDROME SON

To parents considering this option, Rhonda advises, "I would recommend afterschooling if that is the *only* option available. Better yet, I would recommend never sending any child to school." Even though her twelve-year-old son is the one with special needs, Rhonda has decided that homeschooling would also benefit her ten-year-old daughter and vows that her five-year-old son also will never see the inside of a school building.

ENJOY THE BENEFITS

BE SURE TO remind yourself of the academic benefits of educating your children at home. Other important benefits include the rewards that are *not* measured by tests or other formal assessments. Every family participating in this book cited the overall emotional benefits to their children and families. Arnold in California reflects on his eighteen-year-old son's two years of homeschooling: "The rise in his confidence and self-esteem after successfully dealing with academic problems at home, which he had considered insurmountable in the classroom, made all the effort, on everyone's part, wonderfully worthwhile." He adds, "It brought us closer together as a family, and maybe also closer to solving his learning problems." Arnold's son is currently studying computer graphics at a community college, after having successfully passed his state's high school proficiency exam.

Rhonda finds solace in witnessing her son's emotional and academic growth. "I love his newfound confidence with other people, both adults and kids. It means that basically he's become a social person. He's jumped dramatically in reading ability, and now, for the first time in his life, my son loves learning! More than anything," she continues, "we have a child who no longer wants to end his own life. We are blessed beyond belief and very grateful to everyone who paved the way so that homeschooling would be possible."

Consider the not-so-apparent benefits—think toward your child's future. California homeschooling father Robert stresses that

SMALL MIRACLES

I expected it to be very difficult. At first, we worked hard to make everything adjust, so it did work. Now, it just feels good, and the kids have more input in how we homeschool. Expect it to be a challenge, and then anything less than that is great.

—LINDA IN SOUTHERN CALIFORNIA, PARENT TO TWO SONS,
A TWELVE-YEAR-OLD DYSLEXIC AND HIS NINE-YEAR-OLD BROTHER

children only have one opportunity at childhood, and as parents, we should be taking every opportunity to influence the various life factors faced by our children. He notes, "I realize that we cannot protect them from all the difficulties in life, but we can contribute to what shapes their impressions about themselves. If a person feels secure about himself (without becoming a complete narcissist), then he has probably the most important tool toward becoming a productive member of society. That's what I want for my son."

THIS IS YOUR FAMILY'S DECISION

ALL THE PARENTS who contributed to this book urge prospective homeschoolers to do what is best for *their* individual family's needs. Your reasons for deciding to homeschool are uniquely yours, with the bottom line being your child's emotional, physical, and mental welfare.

No other person can provide you with the final answer of whether you should homeschool your children. You'll need to assess your abilities—emotionally and financially—then make the determination on your own. This isn't to say that your decision-making processes must be made in a vacuum. On the contrary, find local support groups, join homeschooling e-mail lists, read the personal Web site accounts of other families who've chosen to educate their children at home. Ask, observe, and read!

This book is your own personal support group. Absorb the comments of other parents when you need encouragement or grounding to remind you of why you're considering or have already started homeschooling your differently abled child. You're not alone on this journey, and the path is well traveled.

Homeschooling can create both wonderful and chaotic changes in your life. True, the challenges can be numbing. You'll have days when you're certain you must've lost your mind deciding to homeschool. Then you recall that first time your child threw her arms around your neck and blurted out, "You're the best teacher ever!"

You possess the ability, knowledge, determination, and love to direct your child's future. You've taken that difficult first step toward empowering your family's growth. Homeschooling is a series of forward paces, dotted by occasional stumbles. For now, you need only grasp opportunity in one hand, your child in the other, and never look back.

INDEX

ABOUT THE AUTHOR

*L*enore Colacion Hayes is the director of a private independent study program in California. Her graduate degree is in community/clinical psychology, with an emphasis in educational psychology. She has been a counselor at both the elementary and college levels. She resides with her husband and always-homeschooled son in Long Beach, California.

Up-to-Date Answers to All Your Homeschooling Questions

More and more families today are turning to homeschooling to teach their children. But where do they go to find honest, practical answers to questions such as: Can I afford it? Or, how will my child make friends without going to school? Look no further. This invaluable guidebook—completely updated to include the 101 most important homeschooling concerns—answers all those questions and more. Inside, you'll learn:

- Methods of motivating, teaching, and testing homeschooled children
- The latest on the growing use of distance-learning tools
- Ways to homeschool your special-needs child
- The differences between homeschooling younger children and teenagers

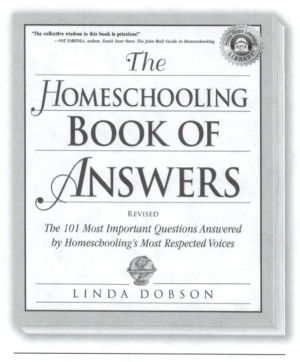

ISBN 0-7615-3570-5 / Paperback / 384 pages
U.S. $16.95 / Can. $25.95

New Ways to Build Trust Between You and Your Child

Are you tired of saying "no"? This empowering book provides you with proven steps and principles for better communication that will help you turn misbehavior into an opportunity to build a stronger trust between you and your child. It's easy to learn, easy to stick to, and you'll be a better parent who raises a more well-adjusted child. With this successful approach, you'll learn how to:

- Motivate your child to listen better
- Teach basic reasoning skills
- Focus on behavioral solutions, not parent-child conflict
- Help your child make connections between choices and consequences
- Learn how to set limits

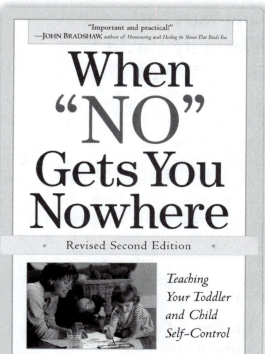

ISBN 0-7615-3480-6 / Paperback / 192 pages
U.S. $12.95 / Can. $19.95

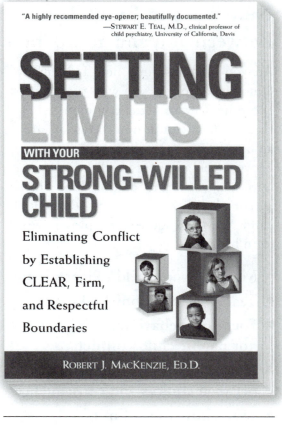